THE
CUISINART
GRIDDLER
COOKBOOK

"Delicious and healthy meals for those of us on the go."

Sarah Swanson

It's a fact: readers who follow an ACTION GUIDE as they read and use cookbooks tend to have the most success!

Here's what I'm going to do to thank you for downloading my book. Go to the link below to instantly sign up for these bonuses.

Here's just a taste of what subscribers get:

Printable Kitchen Guides:

- Keep your food fresher for longer with the Extra-Long Food Storage Guide
- No more guess work in the kitchen -- Metric Conversion Guide
- Make delicious spreads in minutes -- Easy Spreads Guide
- Protect your family from consuming undercooked meat -- Meat Grilling Guide
- Many more new upcoming high-quality guides

Books and Recipes:

- New mouth-watering recipes you have NEVER tried before
- New books I publish for FREE

GRAB YOUR FREEBIES NOW AT
COOKINGWITHAFOODIE.COM

WHY USE THE CUISINART GRIDDLER

It's not just a griddler. It's a full grill, a panini press, quesadilla maker, and a life-saver!

So you're the proud new owner of a Cuisinart Griddler. Seriously, it's not just a griddler. It's the most versatile machine in your kitchen and it promises to make your life easier. This book will help you keep using your griddler so that you never run out of delicious ideas to make. Think it's just for sandwiches and eggs?

Think again! This fantastic machine has way more sneaky uses than you realized. With very little planning, you can throw a complete meal together in very little time!

So what can the Cuisinart Griddler do for you?

- Cleanup is a dream — remove plates & rinse with soap and water! Clean the drip tray. Done
- Cooks meat fast...really fast — seriously, do NOT walk away!
- Grill inside when the weather outside sucks!
- Avoid nasty grease splatters with our guide on choosing the right meats.
- Save time making filling meals quickly

Ok, you probably don't care about all the specifics of this grill. Let's get onto to the good eating!

WHO THIS BOOK IS FOR

This book is for the student who is late for class and still didn't eat breakfast.

This book is for the busy mom who has to feed her kids, husband, AND still get ready for a full day.

This book is for anyone who is constantly "on the go".

No more making excuses for eating unhealthy crap because we're "too busy."

WHAT NOT TO USE THIS GRIDDLER FOR

Let's face it. There are some things that this grill just wasn't designed to make. There are always sneaky tactics we can take….but some things are just best left alone.

For example, this machine just won't do justice to thick-cut meats like steak. Why would you want to ruin such a fine piece of meat anyway? That doesn't mean that you can never cook steak in it. Hell, that's probably why most of you even purchased this grill. Some people have reported that really thick cuts of meat tend to cook unevenly, so use this knowledge to your advantage!

The trick is to beat down these thick cuts with a wooden mallet to allow heat to transfer through the thick meat easier and more evenly.

And you should also avoid fatty meats while you're at it. Many people have complained that the grease tray doesn't do a good job containing the oily sludge. But most of these problems can be solved by using leaner cuts of meat as well as tenderly beating down the thick cuts into thinner pieces.

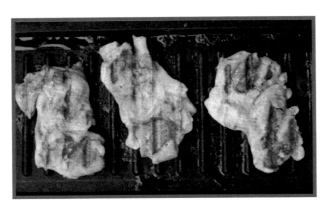

HOW TO PREVENT THE GRIDDLER COATING FROM PEELING…

Yes, this is a problem that some people have reported. You don't want to get these tiny shavings in your food, so the best way to avoid this issue is to avoid using forks and knives to scrape the surface of the metal plates.

The best way to clean it is to use scrub pads that won't scratch or damage the coating on the surface. Scrubbers designed to clean glassware, like the "Scotch Brite No Scratch Scrub Pad" (the blue one) are ideal for cleaning.

TABLE OF CONTENTS

Red Meat

Seafood

Veggie Paninis

Breakfasts

Ultimate Quesadillas

Ultimate Desserts

Ultimate Sides

PLANNING AHEAD

Sometimes, it seems like no amount of preparation or whole nights spent in our kitchens will get us anywhere. So much planning and cooking, and for what? An okay meal, and a really big mess. Not anymore! In this book, I'll help you:

Plan shopping ahead, with a list of the must-have ingredients for the majority of the recipes found in this book.

Get in the habit of planning and freezing for easy, nearly no-chopping meal preparation.

Follow recipes for new and amazingly simple dishes that you'll love, and that require no more than a couple free hours on a Sunday or some free time in the morning.

FREEZE N' THROW

To make your preparation time in the mornings even shorter, set aside ten minutes each weekend to plan ahead your shopping list (for any ingredients that you don't already have ready). This way, you won't be frazzled Monday morning when, half-way through a recipe, you realize you don't have any coconut milk. It's the worst. We've all done it.

To make things even easier on yourself, go ahead and chop up the veggies that you'll need for the week and freeze them! Whether in plastic baggies or resealable plastic containers, it'll be a breeze in the mornings to take what you need out of the freezer, measure it out, and throw it on the grill. That's it!

Now, all that's left to do is start! Life is busy and chaotic, but cooking dinner doesn't have to be. With a little planning, a little grilling, and a lot of delicious and satisfying meals, eating healthful meals won't be difficult ever again.

COMMONLY USED INGREDIENTS

Here's a list of the most commonly used ingredients in this cookbook. Keep your fridge stocked with them chopped and ready to go and you will easily cut down your cooking time by HALF.

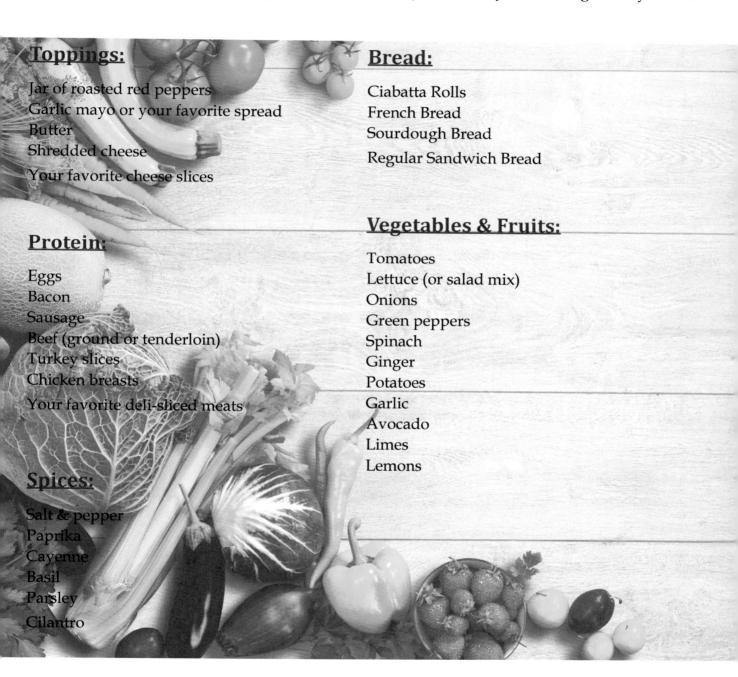

Toppings:

Jar of roasted red peppers
Garlic mayo or your favorite spread
Butter
Shredded cheese
Your favorite cheese slices

Protein:

Eggs
Bacon
Sausage
Beef (ground or tenderloin)
Turkey slices
Chicken breasts
Your favorite deli-sliced meats

Spices:

Salt & pepper
Paprika
Cayenne
Basil
Parsley
Cilantro

Bread:

Ciabatta Rolls
French Bread
Sourdough Bread
Regular Sandwich Bread

Vegetables & Fruits:

Tomatoes
Lettuce (or salad mix)
Onions
Green peppers
Spinach
Ginger
Potatoes
Garlic
Avocado
Limes
Lemons

Painless pantry stocking guide

This guide will help make grocery shopping quick and painless. Stock your pantry with only the best items, and always get the best deals.

Bulk Stores (Costco, Sam's Club, etc)	Natural Groceries (Trader Joe's)	Supermarkets
Frozen organic berries	Deli-sliced meat	Organic veggies
Frozen natural sausage	Canned salmon	Organic free-range eggs
Frozen seafood	Canned tuna	Free-range poultry
Bananas	Frozen fish	Grass-fed beef
Avocados	Avocados	Deli-sliced meat
Deli-sliced meats	Condiments: Mustard, ketchup	High-quality cheeses
Organic almond butter, peanut butter	Trail mix, nuts, and dried fruit	Fermented foods (sauerkraut)
Bagged nuts (almonds, pistachios, walnut)	Olive Oil	Unpasteurized butter (Kerrygold)
Coconut oil	Frozen fruit	Organic heavy cream
Produce (spinach, salad mix, lettuce, etc)	Seasonal produce	Rotisserie chicken
Canned beans, diced tomatoes,	Seasonal fruit	Coconut aminos
Bagged salad	Organic bananas	Yogurt
Ground coffee	Coconut milk	
Almond milk	100% Fruit juice	
Coconut milk	Mushrooms	
	Salami	
	Smoked salmon	

QUICK SPREADS GUIDE

cookingwithafoodie.com

Each spread needs a base to hold all the ingredients together. Many of the ingredients in these recipes can be swapped.

HOW TO USE THIS GUIDE:

1. Choose your base and spices.
2. Add all the ingredients into a food processor and blend well.
3. When adding oil, pour in a slow steady stream as everything is blending.

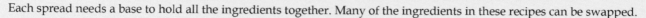

The base holds all the ingredients together and affects the consistency of the spread.

BASE ✚ SPICES ➖ SPREAD

oil / mayo / greek yogurt / plain yogurt
butter / sour cream / cream cheese / egg yolks

SENSATION	BASE	INGREDIENTS	SPREAD
Spicy	1/2 cup whipped cream cheese	1 4oz jar pimientos, 1/2 cup shredded cheddar cheese, 1 tbsp mustard, 25 splashes tobasco	Pimiento Cheese
	1/4 cup mayo	1/2 tsp sriracha, 1/2 tsp. fresh lime juice, 4 drops sesame oil, 1/2 tsp sesame seeds	Spicy Sesame Mayo
	1/3 cup mayo	3/4 cup crumbled blue cheese, 3 tbsp buffalo sauce, 1 tbsp plain yogurt or sour cream, 1/4 tsp granulated sugar, 2 sliced scallions	Buffalo Blue Cheese
	8 oz feta cheese	1/4 cup olive oil, 6 oz jar roasted red peppers, 1/2 tsp red pepper flakes,	Spicy Feta and Red Pepper
	1/3 cup sour cream	3 cups shredded sharp cheddar cheese, 1/3 cup white wine, 4 tbs horseradish, black pepper, 1 tsp paprika	Cheddar Horseradish Spread
	1/4 cup greek yogurt	1 tbsp minced jalapeno, 1 tbsp minced cilantro, 1 tsp lime juice, salt + pepper	Jalapeno-Cilantro Yogurt
Tangy	4 oz goat cheese	parsley, lemon zest, salt + pepper, olives	Parsley + Olive Goat Cheese
	4 oz cream cheese	1 cup crumbled feta, 3 tbs chopped rosemary, 2 tbs lemon juice, 1 minced garlic clove, salt + pepper	Rosemary, Lemon, & Feta
	1 cup mayo, 1/2 cup sour cream	1 cucumber, 1 tsp dried parsley, 1 tsp dried dill weed, 1/2 tsp garlic powder, 1/2 tsp onion powder, 1/4 cup chopped chives, salt + pepper	Ranch Cucumber Dip

SENSATION	BASE	INGREDIENTS	SPREAD
Tangy	1 Hass avocado, 1 cup sour cream	1/2 cup buttermilk, lemon juice, 1 clove minced garlic, 1/4 cup chopped chives, 1/4 cup chopped dill, 1/4 cup chopped parsley, salt + pepper	Tangy Avocado Ranch Sauce
	3 tbs plain Greek yogurt	3/4 – 1 cup cilantro leaves, 1 cloves garlic, 3 tablespoons olive oil, 1 teaspoon honey, 2 teaspoons fresh lime juice	Creamy Cilantro Lime Dressing
	1/2 cup greek yogurt	1 tsp honey, 3 tbs Sriracha sauce	Sweet Sriracha Yogurt
	1/2 cup greek yogurt	1/3 cup lime juice, 1/3 cup olive oil, 1/4 cup water, 2 tbs honey, 1 tbs paprika, 1 tbs cumin, 2 tsp minced garlic, 1 tsp coriander	Southwest Chipotle Lime
	2 cups greek yogurt	4 minced garlic cloves, 1 large diced cucumber, 1 tbs chopped dill, 1-2 tbs lemon juice, 1 tbs olive oil, salt + pepper	Tzatziki
	1 stick unsalted soft butter	3 tbsp fresh chives, 1/2 tsp sea salt	Chive Butter with Sea Salt
	1/2 cup salted butter	1/4 cup chopped basil, 1 minced garlic clove, 1/2 tsp lemon zest, 1/4 tsp black pepper	Lemon Basil Garlic Butter
Sweet	1 cup mayo	1 tbs butter, 1/2 lb diced sweet onion, 2 tbs cider vinegar, 2 tbs honey, 1 tbs mustard, salt + pepper	Sweet Onion Sauce
	2 sticks butter	1/4 cup powdered sugar, 1/4 cup honey, 2 teaspoons cinnamon	Creamy Cinnamon Butter
	1/4 cup coconut oil, melted	20-25 crumbled cookies, 4 T powdered sugar, 1 T brown sugar, 1/4 tsp. vanilla, 1/2 tsp. cinnamon, 1/8 tsp. nutmeg, 3-4 T water	Cookie Butter
	5 ounces cream cheese	caramel sauce (homemade or store-bought), toffee bits	Caramel Apple Cream Cheese

SENSATION	BASE	INGREDIENTS	SPREAD
	8oz low fat cream cheese, soft	½ cup canned pure pumpkin, 4 T ground cinnamon, 4 tsp. ground ginger, 4 tsp. ground nutmeg, 3 tsp. ground allspice, 1 tsp vanilla, 2 tbsp brown sugar, dash of salt	Pumpkin Spice Cream Cheese
Healthy	1 ripe avocado	6 tsp. minced chives, 4 tsp minced parsley, 1 tbsp white wine vinegar, salt + pepper	Herbed Avocado Spread
	3/4 cup ricotta cheese	2 tbsp finely chopped chives, 1 tbsp lemon juice, 1 tbsp parsley, 1 tbsp Parmesan cheese, 2 tsp chopped basil, salt + pepper	Herbed Ricotta Spread
	1/2 cup ricotta cheese	1 cup sun-dried tomatoes, 1 tsp balsamic vinegar, basil leaves, black pepper	Sundried Tomato
	1/4 cup EVOO	3/4 cup shelled walnuts, 2 cups aurugla, 1 tsp red wine vinegar, 1 tsp dijon mustard, salt + pepper,	Arugula Walnut Pesto
	1/2 cup EEVO	3 garlic cloves, 2 cups chopped basil leaves, 1/2 cup grated Parmesan cheese, 1/2 cup pine nuts, salt + pepper	Basic Basil Pesto
	10 oz chick peas	1/4 cup lemon juice, 1/4 cup tahini, 1 chopped garlic, 2 tbs olive oil,	Homemade Hummus
	8 oz feta	3 tbsp olive oil, 4 tsp minced mint, 1 tsp lemon zest, 1/2 tsp black pepper	Whipped Feta Spread
	1/3 cup greek yogurt	2 avocados diced, 1 tbs lemon juice, 1 minced garlic clove, salt + pepper	Creamy Avocado
	1 cup greek yogurt, 8 oz reduced fat cream cheese	2 tbs butter, 1/2 cup Parmesan cheese, 1 cup chopped artichoke hearts, 1/2 cup jalapenos, 2 cups spinach	Skinny Spinach & Artichoke
	1/2 cup Greek yogurt	3/4 cup mint leaves, 1 medium chopped garlic clove, 1 tsp fresh lemon juice, 1/4 tsp salt	Garlic-Mint Yogurt

ORGANIC WATCHLIST

This shopping guide was created using data from independent studies by the Environmental Working Group (EWG). The last public report published by the Environmental Protection Agency (EPA) was in 2007, even though the 1996 "Consumer Right to Know" law requires that the EPA inform consumers about potential health risks caused by pesticides.

This guide is meant to help you plan your shopping trips and become an educated consumer.

The Dirty Dozen:

These fruits and vegetables have been flagged by independent research groups to contain the highest amount of pesticides.

Vegetables	Fruits
1. Spinach	1. Strawberries
2. Celery	2. Apples
3. Bell peppers	3. Peaches
4. Cucumbers	4. Grapes
5. Potatoes	5. Cherry tomatoes
6. Kale/collard greens	6. Nectarines
7. Summer squash	
8. Hot peppers	

To stay updated on the latest news and reports (including the cleanest produce available to consumers) sign up at

cookingwithafoodie.com

What to Store	Fridge	Freezer	Pantry	Tips
Meats				
Poultry	2 days	4 - 6 months	no	Store in a sealed freezer bag.
Fish	2 days	6 months	no	Store in a sealed freezer bag.
Shellfish	2 days	3 - 4 months	no	Store in a sealed freezer bag.
Chops	3 days	6 months	no	Store in a sealed freezer bag.
Bacon	2 weeks (unopened), 1 week (opened)	1 month	no	Store in original packaging, but place inside a sealed freezer bag.
Roasts	3 days	6 months	no	Store in a sealed freezer bag.
Ground	2 days	4 months	no	Store in a sealed freezer bag.
Steak	3 days	6 months	no	Store in a sealed freezer bag.
Sausage (raw)	2 days	2 months	no	Store in a sealed freezer bag.
Garden Vegetables				
Onions	4 days (cut)	3 - 6 months	2 months	Peel, chop and store in a sealed freezer bag.
Peppers	5 - 7 days, 3 - 5 days (cut)	6 - 9 months	no	Wash, chop and store in a sealed freezer bag.
Sweet potatoes	3 days (cut)	2 - 3 months	2 weeks	Peel, dice and store in a sealed freezer bag. Store cooked mashed sweet potatoes in an airtight container.
Mushrooms	1 - 2 weeks	no	no	Store them in a brown paper bag. If they dry out, transfer them to a zip loc bag and add a little warm water before use to restore flavor.
Green leafy vegetables (spinach, kale, etc.)	5 - 7 days	no	no	Store in a perforated bag in the coolest part of your fridge.
Fresh herbs	3 - 5 days	1 - 2 months	1 - 3 days	Mince herbs finely and store in an airtight container.

What to Store	Fridge	Freezer	Pantry	Tips
Fruits				
Bananas	2 weeks	8 - 12 months	5 - 7 days	Peel and store 4 bananas per freezer bag
Tomatoes	"3 - 5 days, 1 - 2 days (cut)"	no	3 - 4 days	
Apples	up to 2 months	8 - 12 months	3 - 5 days	Slice up and add lemon juice to prevent browning. Store in a sealed freezer bag.
Grapes	1-2 weeks	8 - 12 months	no	Wash thoroughly and pat dry. Store in a sealed freezer bag.
Berries	2-7 days	8 - 12 months	no	Wash thoroughly and pat dry. Store in a sealed freezer bag.
Cherries	3 days	8 - 12 months	no	Wash thoroughly and pat dry. Remove pits and store in a sealed freezer bag.
Peaches, plums, nectarines	5 days	6 - 12 months	1 - 3 days	Peel, remove pits and cut into slices. Store in a sealed freezer bag.
Melons	5 days (3 if cut)	6 - 12 months	3 - 4 days	Slice into cubes without rind. Store in a sealed freezer bag.
Baking Goods				
Baked breads (muffins/ banana bread)	3 - 4 days	1 - 2 months	no	Store in sealed freezer bags or an airtight container.
Yeast breads	1 - 2 days	2 - 5 months	no	Store in sealed freezer bags or an airtight container.
Coconut flour	6 months	12 months	no	Store in sealed freezer bags or an airtight container.
Almond flour	6 months	12 - 18 months	no	Store in sealed freezer bags or an airtight container.
Starches	6 - 8 months	12 - 18 months	1 - 2 months	Store in sealed freezer bags or an airtight container.

What to Store	Fridge	Freezer	Pantry	Tips
Cookies	1 week	3 months	3 - 4 days	Store in sealed freezer bags or an airtight container.
Misc				
Dried fruits	no	no	6 months (unopened)	no
Nuts, seeds	6 - 12 months	1 - 2 years	1 month	Remove shells first. Store in a sealed freezer bag or an airtight container.
Shredded coconut	8 - 12 months	12 - 18 months	6 months (unopened)	Store in a sealed freezer bag.
Homemade broth	5 - 7 days	3 months	no	Store in an sealed freezer bag or an airtight container. Leave room for expansion when liquid freezes.
Butter (sticks)	3 months	6 months	no	Store in original packaging and place inside a sealed freezer bag.
Ghee	9 - 12 months	12 - 18 months	6 months (unopened)	Store in an airtight container.
Coconut milk, canned	7 - 10 days	2 - 4 months	1 - 2 years (unopened)	Store in an sealed freezer bag or an airtight container. Leave room for expansion when liquid freezes.

GRILLED CHEESE

Ultimate Grilled Cheese

Warm Broccoli & Cheddar

"Loaded Nacho" Southwestern Grilled Cheese

French Onion Grilled Cheese

Warm Broccoli & Cheddar

What could be better than starting the day off with this deliciously hot cheese and broccoli grilled sandwich? Add chicken breast deli slices for an easy protein boost.

Directions:

1. Chop up the broccoli into tiny pieces and add in with 2 tbsps of butter in a frying pan. Mix well.
2. Slice up the garlic and onion and add with the broccoli in the pan. Cook until all the vegetables get nice and tender.
3. Preheat the grill to medium heat.
4. Just as the broccoli is about done, throw in 2 shredded slices of chicken breast meat. Mix well.
5. Spread a little butter on the outside of two slices of bread. Add the broccoli and cheddar filling and close the sandwich.
6. Set the sandwich in the grill and close the lid, cooking for (3-5 min), or until it is nice and toasted.

Ingredients:

2 Slices French Bread
1 Slice of Yellow Onion
4-5 small pieces of Broccoli
2 Slices Chicken Breast Deli Meat
1/2 Clove Garlic
2 Slices of Cheddar Cheese
Butter
Salt
Pepper

"Loaded Nacho" Southwestern Grilled Cheese

Watch out for this grilled cheese! Loaded with classic Southwestern ingredients, it will sidekick your tastebuds and bust your hunger. The crushed Doritos add an excellent flavorful crunch.

Ingredients:

2 slices french bread
1 tbsp sour cream
2 tbsp salsa
Tex mex cheese
½ cup cooked ground beef
1/8 tsp taco seasoning
1 Green onion stalk, chopped
4-5 cilantro leaves
1 Slice of tomato, diced
1/4 Avocado, diced
1-2 Black olives, chopped
1 Tbsp black bean
1-2 Slices jalapeno pepper, chopped
1-2 Handful nacho flavoured Doritos crushed
1 Egg, scrambled
Butter

Directions:

1. Crack the egg into a bowl large enough for dipping. Dip only one side of a bread slice in the egg and place face down on the plate of Doritos to make them stick. Repeat with the next slice.
2. Preheat the grill to medium heat.
3. Add sour cream to the top slice and salsa to the bottom slice.
4. Next, add a layer of cheese on the bottom slice, cooked beef, taco seasoning, chopped onion, diced tomatoes, black beans, jalapeno peppers, olives, and diced avocado.
5. Add the sandwich to the grill and press down the lid, sealing the sandwich (make sure everything didn't fall out).
6. Cook the sandwich until the cheese is nice and melty and the bread is toasted (4-6 min).

The Ultimate Grilled Cheese

Oh my! This is the meltiest and cheesiest sandwich you will ever try. Grilled to perfection — crunchy on the outside, chewy and soft on the inside. Caution: you might have to slap some hands away.

Directions:

1. Preheat the grill to medium.
2. Butter each slice of french bread and spread mayo also.
3. Place the three slices of cheese and tomato slices in between the bread halves.
4. Set the sandwich in the grill and close the lid.

Cook for 2-3 minutes or until the sandwich is lightly toasted and the cheese is melty. Serve with fresh fruit for a nice twist.

Ingredients:

2 pieces of french bread

1 tsp of butter

1/4 tsp of salt

2-3 tbsps of Mayo

3 slices of Sharp Cheddar, Colby-Jack and Fontina – one of each (or mix your favorite cheeses)

2 Slices of fresh tomato

French Onion Grilled Cheese

Every once in a while, we get those cravings for something gooey, cheesy, and melty. Eating out often is not always the best choice, so here's a healthier alternative you can make yourself. The combination of nutty Gruyere cheese and caramelized onions is exquisite. Just like French onion soup.

Ingredients:

2 medium yellow onions, sliced thin

3 tbsps butter softened

3 tbsps white wine

4.5 oz gruyere cheese, shredded

4 slices sourdough bread

salt and freshly ground pepper

Directions:

1. Melt some butter in a pan and add the sliced onions. Stir until onions start to brown, (3-4 minutes). Season with salt and pepper.

2. Spread onions in an even layer, cover pot, and reduce heat to low. Stir every 5 or so minutes. Continue until onions are nice and brown and caramelized (15-20 min). *The length of this process depends on how many onions you use.*

3. Increase heat to medium-high, add the wine to deglaze the pan, and scrape up any brown bits from the bottom. Turn the heat off once all the liquid has absorbed (about 2-3 min).

4. Preheat grill to medium heat. Butter both sides of bread and add cheese, caramelized onions, and more cheese on top of the onions.

5. Cook until cheese is melted and the outside is toasted golden brown.

FREE-RANGE POULTRY

The Day After Thanksgiving

Garlic Chicken Panini

Sundried Tomato Pesto & Goat Cheese Chicken Panini

Lemongrass Chicken

Grilled Tandoori Chicken

Homemade Chicken Tenders

Basil Lemon Chicken Salad

Cali Avocado Chicken Crunch

Sun-Dried Tomato Pesto & Goat Cheese Chicken Panini

A fantastic way to use up leftover grilled chicken, this sandwich is a winner. The distinct flavor of goat cheese is much stronger than typical cheeses. You will love the mix of juicy sun-dried tomato pesto and rich goat cheese.

Ingredients:

Leftover rotisserie chicken

¼ to ½ cup fresh goat cheese

¼ to ½ cup sun-dried tomato pesto

1-2 cups organic arugula

2 slices gluten-free whole grain bread

Directions:

1. Preheat the grill to medium heat.
2. Spread 1-2 tbsps of goat cheese on one slice of the bread.
3. Spread 1-2 tbsps of sun-dried tomato pesto on the other slice.
4. Top the goat cheese with some of the organic arugula and place the leftover chicken over the slice with sun-dried tomato pesto. Close the sandwich.
5. Brush outer surface of the sandwiches with olive oil.
6. Close the lid and cook until golden. Remove from heat and serve.

Buffalo Chicken

If you are obsessed with the flavor of buffalo wing sauce over chicken, then this is for you. Melty mozzarella and blue cheese drizzled with mild or spicy buffalo sauce — its super easy and quick to make.

Directions:

1. Preheat the grill to medium-high heat.
2. Mix the chicken, bleu cheese and buffalo sauce in bowl.
3. Add the filling between two slices of bread with cheese included.
4. Set the sandwich on the grill and press down the lid.
5. Cook for 3-5 min, or until the panini is nice and toasted.

Ingredients:

two slices of bread
½ chicken breast shredded
¼ cup buffalo chicken sauce
¼ cup of blue cheese
two slices of mozzarella

The Sonny Falconi

Yes, it sounds like an Italian mobster. But you have nothing to fear! This harmless panini is not only delicious, but strangely tantalizing. Put out a hit on your hunger and show your stomach who's boss. Bon appetit!

Ingredients:

2 tbsps unsalted butter

3 medium red onions, halved and sliced thinly

Salt and pepper

4 fully-cooked chicken-apple sausage links (such as Aidell's)

8 ounces Fontina cheese, shredded

Garlic mayo

1 ciabatta roll, divided into 4 sections, or 4 small ciabatta rolls

Directions:

1. Preheat the grill to medium.
2. Melt the butter in a large skillet over medium heat. Caramelize the onions and season with salt and pepper for 10-15 min, stirring occasionally.
3. Slice the chicken-apple sausage link in half on its longest side but don't cut all the way through.
4. Place the open side of the sausage on the grill and close the lid.
5. Grill the sausages for 4 to 5 min until they are heated through and grill marks appear.
6. Take two ciabatta rolls and sprinkle cheese over one half and spread the garlic mayo over the other.
7. Now add the grilled sausage and caramelized onions and close the sandwich.
8. Press down the lid and grill the panini until the cheese is melted and the bread is toasted, about 4 to 5 min. Cut in half and serve immediately

The Classic Turkey, Bacon and Swiss

It's all in the name — turkey, bacon and swiss. With just a few simple ingredients, you can whip up an easy and tasty panini. Who knew these three ingredients would make such a delectable treat?

Directions:

1. Preheat the grill to medium heat.
2. Spread butter on two slices of bread.
3. Flip over one slice of bread and top it with a few spoonfuls of garlic basil mayo, turkey, bacon and cheese.
4. Close the sandwich with the other slice of bread.
5. Grill two paninis at a time, with the lid closed, until the cheese is melted and the bread is toasted (4-5 min).

Ingredients:

4 tbsps butter
8 slices sourdough bread
8 slices of turkey breast
8 strips of cooked bacon
4 slices of Swiss cheese
garlic basil mayo

Roasted Turkey Jalapeño Melty

If you have leftover turkey slices or a nice roasted turkey sitting in the fridge, this is the perfect sandwich to make. Pack it on with more jalapeños to really kick up the spice.

Ingredients:

8 slices sourdough bread
4 slices Monterey Jack cheese
Sliced pickled jalapeño peppers
Leftover roast turkey (sliced or
    shredded)
1-2 tomatoes (thin slices)
Mayo

Directions:

1. Preheat the grill to medium-high heat.
2. Add a slice of cheese, jalapeños, leftover turkey and tomatoes.
3. Spread a thin layer of mayonnaise on the other slice of bread and close the sandwich.
4. Close the lid and grill until the cheese is melty and the bread is toasted (4-5 min).

Turkey Meatball Parmesan

This is a great twist on the traditional meatball parmesan sub. The turkey meatballs are a much healthier choice over sausage meatballs. Warm, tender, and super simple.

Directions:

1. Preheat the grill to medium heat.
2. Spoon 2-3 tbsp. of butter onto the grill plates and add the meatballs. Close the lid and cook for 5-7 min.
3. Remove the meatballs when they start browning to a plate.
4. Fill the sub rolls with the meatballs, marinara and mozzarella cheese and set on grill. Close lid gently without crushing the rolls for 2-3 min.
5. Sprinkle with parmesan before eating.

Ingredients:

Spicy turkey meatballs (sliced in half)
1 cup marinara
4 6-in sub rolls
2 tbsp. parmesan cheese
8 oz. mozzarella cheese

Deluxe Turkey Apple Cheddar

How do you turn a regular turkey sandwich into a deluxe version? Easy. You slip in some slices of sharp cheddar, crisp tart apple, and hearty whole-grain bread — then toast them all together.

Ingredients:

4 slices whole grain bread
4 tbsps butter
2 tbsp Dijon mustard
1 green apple thinly sliced
8 slices sharp cheddar cheese
8 thin slices deli roasted turkey

Directions:

1. Preheat the grill.
2. Spread the outside of each slice of bread with a tbsp of butter.
3. Spread mustard evenly over two slices of bread. Layer with apple slices, cheese and turkey. Top each with the remaining bread slices.
4. Press down the lid and grill each sandwich for 3-5 minutes, or until bread is nice and toasted and the cheese has melted. Remove from pan, cut in half and serve immediately.

Cilantro Chicken with Lime

So you want a healthy alternative to greasy fatty meats? There's something about cilantro chicken that brings the whole family together. With a few splashes of lime, this dish promises to curb your hunger with a one-two protein-packed punch. And its insanely delicious!

Directions:

1. Drop the chicken thighs in a large bowl or Ziploc bag.
2. Zest the limes over the chicken
3. Squeeze the lime juice into the chicken.
4. Now throw in the cilantro, garlic, honey, olive oil, salt and pepper. Be sure to completely cover the meat.
5. Let the chicken marinate for about 30 minutes at room temperature, or in the fridge overnight. Let the chicken thaw to room temperature before cooking.
6. Preheat broiler or grill. Once its ready, set the thighs on the rack and sprinkle with coriander. Cook 5–6 minutes per side.

Ingredients:

2 pounds boneless, skinless chicken thighs
2 limes
½ cup fresh cilantro
6 cloves garlic
1 tbsp honey
1 tbsp olive oil
¼ to ½ teaspoon salt and pepper
1 teaspoon ground coriander

Spicy Garlic Basil Turkey Sausage

Voila! Another healthy alternative to your favorite unhealthy meaty foods. These turkey sausages can be prepared in less than 10 minutes, then frozen or cooked right away. If you find that you're running in and out the door during workdays, keep a stash of cooked sausages in the freezer. They make a tasty lunch or afternoon snack.

Ingredients:

- 1.3 pounds ground turkey (a 20-ounce package is fine as well)
- 1 tbsp chopped fresh basil or 1 teaspoon dried basil
- 1 teaspoon crushed garlic
- 1 teaspoon fine sea salt
- 1 teaspoon sweet paprika
- 1/4 teaspoon black pepper
- 1/8 to 1/4 teaspoon cayenne pepper, the more the spicier

Directions:

1. Preheat the grill medium-high heat.
2. In a large mixing bowl, combine the turkey, garlic, paprika, basil, salt, pepper, and cayenne.
3. Using your hands to create 8 equal-sized patties.
4. Spoon a little butter or oil onto the grill plates and set the patties. (If you want to make all 8, use the full grill — but flip them after 5-6 min)
5. Alternatively, close the lid and grill for 4-5 min, or until browned.

Avocado, Turkey & Goat Cheese

Need that blast of nutrition in the morning to get you going? Combined with healthy fats from avocado and a boost of protein from lean turkey, you're sure to feel great and energetic after this meal.

Directions:

1. Preheat grill to medium-high heat.
2. Spread goat cheese on one slice of bread and add the turkey, arugula and avocado to the other one.
3. Close the sandwich and set on the grill.
4. Grill the sandwich for 3-5 min, or until it is nice and toasted.

Ingredients:

2 slices of sourdough bread

1 handful arugula

Half a ripe avocado, sliced

3 slices of oven-roasted deli turkey meat

1-2 tbsps goat cheese

Salt & pepper

Basil Lemon Chicken Salad

Chicken salad is a classic sandwich anyone can enjoy! This basil lemon version is zesty, very hearty, and super flavorful.

Ingredients:

2 lbs boneless skinless chicken
    breasts
2 slices bread
the juice and zest of 1 lemon
1/4 cup basil leaves, chopped
2/3 cup diced red bell pepper
2/3 cup diced celery
1/3 cup diced red onion
1/3 cup mayonnaise
salt and pepper to taste
olive oil

Directions:

1. Preheat the grill to medium heat.
2. Add salt and pepper to chicken breasts. Drizzle olive oil over the grill plates and set chicken on grill.
3. Press the lid down and cook chicken until it is thoroughly cooked and browned on the outside. Remove from grill and cool.
4. Mix the lemon, basil, red bell pepper, celery, red onion and mayonnaise in a large bowl.
5. Chop cooled chicken and add to bowl. Mix thoroughly.
6. Add the chicken salad in between two slices of bread and set in the grill and close the lid once again. Toast the sandwich until the outside is golden brown and the inside is warm.

Homemade Chicken Tenders

Juicy and crispy chicken tenders just like mom used to make. If you have kids, these will be gone fast, so make sure you get to try one first. Tenders are now easier than ever to make with an indoor grill. You won't ever miss the greasy fast food version anymore.

Directions:

1. Pound the chicken breasts to reduce thickness
2. Cut the chicken breasts into medium-sized strips
3. Grab a ziploc bag and throw in the lime juice, honey, salad dressing and chicken strips.
4. Marinate overnight for the best tasting tenders, but at least for 2 hours (unless you're out of time)
5. Preheat your grill on the high heat setting for 4-5 minutes.
6. Set the tenders on the grill plate and space them apart before closing the lid.
7. Grill them for about 4-5 minutes. Be sure to check that they're fully cooked by cutting one in half (it should be white inside).

Ingredients:

1 lb chicken breast tenderloins (or use regular chicken breast cut to size)

1/2 cup Italian salad dressing

Juice of 1 lime

 teaspoons of honey

Lemongrass Chicken

This dish will be a huge favorite to serve up during parties, but it also makes a great appetizer to share on a date. It is perfectly light in flavor — not too spicy, not too sweet — just right. Serve it up on skewers and garnish with cilantro to give it a more elegant look.

Ingredients:

2 stalks lemongrass, peeled and chopped

1 shallot, finely diced

1 clove garlic, chopped

1 teaspoon ginger, grated

1 birds eye chili, seeded and chopped

1 tbsp sugar

1/2 tbsp oyster sauce (or soy sauce)

1 tbsp fish sauce

1 tbsp oil

1 pound chicken breast, cut into 3/4 inch cubes

Directions:

1. Blend the lemongrass, shallot, garlic, ginger and chili into a fine paste.
2. Mix in the sugar, oyster sauce, fish sauce and oil into the lemongrass paste
3. Marinate the chicken for at least an hour, covered in the fridge. (The longer, the better)
4. Preheat the grill to medium-high heat and slide skewers into the chicken.
5. Close the lid until golden brown on both sides, about 3-5 minutes.

Zesty Chicken Bacon Ranch

Do you have a craving for chicken and bacon? Well, get ready to satisfy it in this crunchy version! We combine the power of bacon alongside a few other simple ingredients to bring you the best combination you have ever encountered.

Directions:

1. Preheat grill to medium-high heat.
2. Add bacon strips and press down lid to cook until they are nice and crispy (3-5 min). Remove and set on a towel (chop when cool).
3. Add chicken breasts to grill and press down lid to cook them thoroughly (5-7 min). Slice one open to make sure it is fully cooked. Remove and cut into small pieces.
4. Fill the bread with chicken and bacon pieces. Add ranch dressing and cheese slices on top.
5. Close the sandwich and set in the grill. Press down the lid and grill until the sandwich is nice and toasted (3-5 min).

Ingredients:

1 Tbsp olive oil
4 slices Italian bread
2 Tbsp ranch dressing
4 slices of cheddar cheese
6 strips of bacon
2 small chicken breasts, grilled

Greek Lemon Yogurt & Turkey

The zestiest tasting greek yogurt and turkey combination yet, this panini is sure to please your palette. The subtle flavor of parmigiano reggiano in a distinctly lemon basil greek yogurt dip goes perfectly with the light turkey flavor.

Ingredients:

1/2 tbsp mayo
1/2 tbsp fat-free Greek yogurt
juice from half a lemon
1 tbsp chopped fresh basil
1/2 tbsp grated parmigiano
    reggiano
salt & freshly-ground pepper
2 slices bread
2 ounces oven-roasted deli turkey
1 roma tomato, sliced

Directions:

1. Preheat grill to medium-high heat.
2. Mix in the mayo, yogurt, lemon juice, basil and cheese in a bowl. Season with salt and pepper.
3. Spread the mixture on one slice of bread. Add the turkey and tomato slices on the other half and close the sandwich.
4. Set on the grill and press down the lid for 3-5 minutes, or until it is nice and toasted.

Cheesy Veggie Turkey Roast

In the spirit of keepin' it simple, we still bring you the easy turkey veggie toast. If you're on the go, or need a quick meal to fill you up, you'll love this one. Hearty and healthy in less than 15 minutes!

Directions:

1. Preheat grill to medium-high heat.
2. Mix in the mayo, yogurt, lemon juice, basil and cheese in a bowl. Season with salt and pepper.
3. Spread the mixture on one slice of bread. Add the turkey and tomato slices on the other half and close the sandwich.
4. Set on the grill and press down the lid for 3-5 minutes, or until it is nice and toasted.

Ingredients:

1 Onion, sliced and caramelized
2 Tbsp Butter
4 slices Hearty Garlic Artisan Bread
Mayo
Dijon Mustard
½ pound deli-roast turkey slices
1 Tomato, thinly sliced
1 cup Spinach
Colby jack cheese slices (or your favorite)

The Day After Thanksgiving

Leftover turkey is inevitable after Thanksgiving. Here we bring you a sandwich where you can put all those extra leftovers to good use. Be careful when you sink your teeth into this sandwich, you might be tempted to cook another turkey just for the leftover sandwiches the week after!

Ingredients:

1 tbsp olive oil

1 loaf of French bread, cut into 3-4 equal pieces

1/2 cup pesto

4-8 ounces mozzarella, sliced

2 cups chopped leftover Thanksgiving turkey

2 Roma tomatoes, thinly sliced

1 avocado, halved, pitted and sliced

Directions:

1. Preheat grill to medium-high heat.
2. Spray cooking oil onto the grill plates.
3. Spread 2-3 tbsp. of pesto on one half of the French bread and top with mozzarella, turkey, tomatoes, and avocado slices.
4. Close the sandwich and set on grill.
5. Press down the lid and cook until both sides are brown and toasted (3-5 min).

Cali Chicken Avocado Crunch

Hot and crunchy on the outside, cool and tender on the inside — that is the Californian way. Inspired by West Coast themes, this sandwich is a generous mix of all kinds of crazy ingredients all married into one delicious meal.

Directions:

1. Spread 2 tbsp of pesto on one slice of bread and goat cheese (or cream cheese) on the other slice. Set aside.
2. Add deli-chicken breast slices, bacon strips, tomatoes, avocado, basil leaves, and sprouts. Close the sandwich.
3. Set in grill and toast the sandwich for 3-4 min. Remove and set on plate.
4. Open the sandwich without spilling any of the filling, and stuff it with the potato chips to give your meal a satisfying crunch.

Ingredients:

4 slices of sourdough bread
1/4 cup basil pesto
2 ounces cream cheese or goat cheese, softened
2 ounces blue cheese, crumbled (may sub your favorite cheese)
1 roma tomato, sliced and seasoned with salt & pepper
1 avocado, peeled, pitted & sliced
1/2 cup alfalfa sprouts
4 leaves of fresh basil
Deli-chicken breast slices
4 slices thick cut bacon, cooked
2 handfuls potato chips

Chili Lime Chicken Burgers

Chicken in any form is a favorite, but with chili lime? Hallelujah! Prepared with these instructions, your chicken should come out moist and tender and ready to enjoy with healthy, vitamin-dense vegetables such as roasted asparagus, steamed spinach, or sautéed zucchini and butternut squash.

Ingredients:

1lb ground chicken
2 green onions, chopped
1/4 cup chopped red bell pepper
2 tbsps chopped cilantro
2 teaspoons minced garlic
1/2 teaspoon salt
1/4 teaspoon red pepper flakes
1 lime, cut in half
4 slices pepper jack cheese
4 buns, toasted

For the guacamole:

1 avocado
garlic powder
salt & pepper
diced onions
diced tomatoes

Directions:

To prepare the burgers:

1. Throw in the chicken, green onions, bell pepper, cilantro, garlic, salt, red pepper flakes and lime juice in a large bowl. Mix thoroughly.
2. Form the mixture into 4 even patties and spray each side generously with non-stick spray.
3. Preheat the grill to medium-high. Grill the patties for 3-4 minutes a side, or until cooked all the way through.
4. At the very end, place a slice of cheese on top of each burger, then cover with a large pot lid, and allow to melt for about a minute.
5. Remove burgers to a plate and allow to cool for 5 minutes. Toss it on a toasted bun with your favorite burger toppings.

For the guacamole:

1. Mash all ingredients together with a potato masher or fork.

Grilled Tandoori Chicken

The name tandoori chicken comes from the name of the clay oven the dish is meant to be prepared in. But if you don't have a giant tandoor oven available at home, the Cuisinart grill is a perfect alternative. The longer you let the chicken marinate, the tastier this dish will turn out — seriously, this is important.

Directions:

1. Mix all the ingredients, but the meat, into a bowl.
2. Drop the chicken in a freezer bag along with the marinade and shake well.
3. Marinate in the fridge for at least an hour, preferably several hours to overnight.
4. Pull the freezer bag out of the fridge and let it sit in room temperature.
5. Remove the chicken from the marinade and skewer it.
6. Preheat the grill.
7. Grill the chicken until cooked, about 3-5 minutes per side

Ingredients:

1/2 cup plain yogurt
1/2 lemon (juice)
1/2 small onion (grated)
1 tbsp garlic (grated)
1 tbsp ginger (grated)
1 tbsp garam masala
1 tbsp paprika
1 teaspoon cumin (toasted and ground)
1 teaspoon coriander (toasted and ground)
1/2 teaspoon cayenne pepper
salt to taste
1 pound chicken (boneless and skinless, cut into 1 inch pieces)

Garlic Chicken Panini

There's something about the aroma of garlic and spices that lights up a regular panini. You will be surprised by the powerful combination of chicken, black pepper, garlic, and herbs. In fact, you might end up making another one.

Ingredients:

1/4 cup kosher salt

2 tbsps honey

1 bay leaf

1 crushed garlic clove

6 whole black peppercorns

A dash of dried thyme

A dash of dried parsley

1 quart water

Juice of 1/2 lemon

1 lb. boneless, skinless chicken
    breast cutlets (thin-sliced)

1 baguette, cut into 4 pieces,
    halved lengthwise

Basil garlic mayo

1 small jar of marinated artichoke
    hearts, sliced about 1/4" thick

1 small jar of roasted red peppers

4 slices Swiss cheese

Directions:

Preparing the chicken:
1. Mix the water, honey, salt, garlic, thyme, lemon juice, and parsley into a large bowl.
2. Now throw in the chicken.
3. Cover the bowl and refrigerate for 30-40 minutes.

Cooking the chicken:
1. Preheat the grill to medium-high heat.
2. Grill the marinated chicken breasts for 3-4 minutes until they're cooked thoroughly.
3. Remove the chicken and turn off the grill to wipe it clean.

To make the sandwich:
1. Preheat the grill to medium heat once again
2. Spread a dollop of garlic mayo inside two baguette halves.
3. Place a chicken breast cutlet on the bottom bread half.
4. Arrange layers of artichoke hearts and roasted red peppers over the chicken.
5. Add a slice of cheese and close the sandwich with the top bread half.
6. Press down the lid and grill the sandwich for 4-5 minutes until the cheese is melted and the bread is toasted.

The Not-Such a Jerk Chicken Panini

This version of the classic Jamaican Jerk Chicken is not such a jerk after all. Who gave it such a mean name anyway? You're going to need a lot more ingredients to prepare this awesome panini, but it's absolutely worth it to experience the delightful dance of Jamaican flavors in your mouth. No joke mon'.

Directions:

Marinating the chicken:
1. Blend the following ingredients: rum, vinegar, olive oil, onion, hot peppers, onion, green onion tops, thyme, salt, pepper, allspice, nutmeg, ginger, cinnamon, and molasses into a blender. The consistency should be smooth paste.
2. Drop the chicken in a large freezer bag.
3. Add the lime juice and the jerk paste into the bag. Shake vigorously, making sure to coat the chicken thoroughly.
4. Seal the bag and refrigerate overnight.
5. Making the sandwich
6. Preheat the grill to medium heat.
7. Warm up the pita bread in the microwave on High for about 15-25 sec.
8. Add two slices of cheese in the pita.
9. Add a chicken cutlet and a few spoonfuls of pineapple-black bean salsa and fold the pita.
10. Press down the lid and grill until cheese is nice and melty and grill marks appear (3-4 min).

Ingredients:

cup malt vinegar (or white vinegar)
1 tbsp dark rum
1 jalapeno
1/2 red onion, chopped
2 green onion tops, chopped
1 1/2 teaspoons dried thyme or 1 tbsp fresh thyme leaves, chopped
1 tbsp olive oil
1 teaspoon salt
1 teaspoon freshly ground black pepper
2 teaspoons ground
1/4 allspice
2 teaspoons ground cinnamon
2 teaspoons ground nutmeg
2 teaspoons ground ginger
1 teaspoon molasses
4 boneless, skinless chicken breast cutlets (or 2 chicken breasts cut in half lengthwise)
1/4 cup lime juice
Vegetable oil, for brushing grill grates

RED MEAT

Roast Beef with French Dip

Spicy Italian Panini

Mountain O' Steak

Red Wine Pepper-Glazed Steak

Homemade Mini Meatball Sub

Kimchi Bulgogi Panini

Chili Verde Steak Melty

BBQ Steak & Potato

Red Wine Pepper-Glazed Steak

You will pat yourself on the back after pulling this dish off completely in the comfort of your home. Your friends won't believe you made this yourself. Reward yourself with a glass of red wine. Yeah, its that classy.

Directions:

1. Get out a large saucepan and mix in red wine, peppercorns, Grill Mates seasoning, sugar, salt, and pepper.
2. Let the mixture warm up over medium heat for about 5 minutes, stirring well.
3. Let the sauce cool down and then pour into a big resealable plastic bag.
4. Throw in the steak, seal the bag, and shake vigorously. Refrigerate for at least 1 hour to marinate.
5. Heat the griddler's full grill plates to medium-high. Grill the steak for about 5-8 min if you desire it done medium-rare. Time will depend on thickness of steak, and how you like them cooked.
6. Open the griddler and remove the steaks from the grill. Let them cool for a few minutes to let the sauce absorb into the meat.

Ingredients:

1 cup red wine
1 tbsp black peppercorns
1 tsp McCormick Grill Mates Montreal Steak seasoning (or your favorite)
Pinch of white sugar
Pinch of salt
Dash or two of coarse black pepper

Roast Beef with French Dip

A roast beef sandwich isn't complete without this savory French dip by its side. This is not like the roast beef your mother used to make. The best part is that you get to enjoy various beefy creations throughout the week from one batch in the slow cooker.

Ingredients:

3 lb roast beef
2 cups beef stock
swiss cheese
1 medium white onion (sliced)
1-2 tbsps butter
1 sweet yellow onion, sliced
1/2 cup au jus (beef stock) from
   the cooked roast in the crock
   pot

Directions:

To prepare roast beef:
1. Salt and pepper the beef before browning meat in a frying pan.
2. Combine these ingredients in a slow cooker: 2 cups beef stock, 1 medium white onion, browned beef, and set to cook on high heat for 5 hours.
3. Save the leftover liquid in a bowl (French dip).

To prepare panini:
1. Preheat grill to medium-high heat.
2. Add cooked beef to each bun with a slice of swiss on top and set sandwich on grill. Close lid and cook for 2-3 min.
3. Serve paninis with French dip for dunking.

The Chili Verde Steak Melty

Now this panini is the most interesting flavor your mouth will savor all week. It's not overly spicy, but does sizzle your tongue when combined with the steak and cheese. Oh yeah, it's a mouthful.

Directions:

1. Generously sprinkle salt and pepper over the steak.
2. Preheat the grill to medium-high heat.
3. Add olive oil after a minute, then the steak.
4. Close the lid and let the steak cook to your preferred doneness. For medium, cook it until your instant read thermometer reads 137°F.
5. Remove the steak when its done and set it on a cutting board for 5-10 min.
6. Slice it into thin slices.
7. Cut the bread loaves into two.
8. Spread a tbsp of mayo inside each half of bread.
9. Add a slice of cheese, the steak, onions, chiles and a second slice of cheese on the top.
10. Close the sandwich with the other slice of bread.
11. Press down the lid and grill the panini until the cheese is nice and melty (4-5 min).

Ingredients:

1 pound New York strip steak
Kosher salt and pepper
1 tbsp extra virgin olive oil
Chipotle Mayonnaise
1 ciabatta loaf or baguette, cut
   into 4 sections
8 slices Monterey Jack cheese
Caramelized Onions
1 7-oz can whole roasted green
   chiles, chopped

Mountain O'Steak

The title says it all for this one. If you're a carnivore, you're sure to enjoy this literally mountain of marinated juicy steak, sautéed mushrooms, and bubbly cheese. Vegetarians stay away.

Ingredients:

1 large peeled onion, sliced into five thick slices

1 8-oz package button mushrooms

3 tbsps butter separated (or as needed)

3 tbsps extra virgin olive oil separated (or as needed)

Sugar

1/8 cup bourbon

Salt

Few grinds of pepper

1 tbsp extra virgin olive oil

1 pound shaved steak

¼ pound sliced provolone cheese

Bulkie or Sub rolls

Garlic Aioli, or mayo

Directions:

1. Preheat the grill to medium heat.
2. Spoon 2-3 tbsp. of butter into a large skillet and add the shaved steak, cooking evenly for 6-8 min.
3. Meanwhile, in a medium skillet, melt a tbsp. of butter with 1 tbsp. of Extra Virgin Olive Oil over medium heat.
4. Sauté the onions for 10-12 min until browned and caramelized, stirring occasionally.
5. Add a pinch of salt and pepper, and then a large pinch of sugar. Stir them well.
6. Throw in mushrooms into the mix with another tbsp. of butter.
7. Remove the onions, mushrooms, and steak from the skillets and place them between two sub rolls.
8. Add a slice of provolone cheese and set the sandwich on the grill and close lid.
9. Grill panini for 2-3 min, or until cheese is melted and bread is toasted.
10. Remove to a plate and spread mayo over the top.

Homemade Mini Meatball Sub

Meatball subs are a favorite, and they're a classic sub to eat when you need to fill your belly. This homemade minced beef recipe is loaded with Italian herbs and spices, and packed into a golden-crusted sandwich.

Directions:

To prepare meatballs:
1. Combine the beef, cheese, garlic, basil, bread crumbs, parsley, pepper flakes, salt and pepper into a large bowl. Mix well and form meatballs (1-in. diameter).
2. Preheat the grill to medium-high heat
3. Cook the meatballs in grill until they are all well-browned (7-9 min).

To prepare the paninis:
1. Prepare the bread halves with butter, cooked meatballs, fontina cheese.
2. Close the sandwich and set on grill. Close the lid and cook for 3-5 min, or until panini is nice and toasted.

Ingredients:

2 slices french bread
1 pound lean ground beef
1/3 cup romano cheese
1/4 cup panko bread crumbs
2 garlic cloves, minced
1 teaspoon dried basil
1 teaspoon dried parsley
1/2 teaspoon crushed red pepper flakes
1/2 teaspoon salt
1/2 teaspoon pepper
1 tbsp olive oil
1 (14-ounce) can diced tomatoes
1 tbsp unsalted butter

Spicy Italian Panini

Do you love spicy meats? Attack your senses on all fronts with this super hearty and spicy Italian panini. Served in ciabatta sandwich rolls, this panini is ready to go when you are.

Ingredients:

1/2 cup mayo
1/2 tsp garlic powder
1/4 tsp dried or fresh basil
1/4 lb. deli sliced ham
1/4 lb. deli sliced spicy salami
1/4 lb. deli sliced spicy capicollo
8 (1 oz) slices of provolone
   cheese
1/2 cup jarred, spicy sliced
   pepper rings, drained
1 (10 oz) jar roasted red bell
   pepper strips, drained
4 large ciabatta sandwich rolls,
   split

Directions:

1. Preheat grill to medium-high heat.
2. Combine the mayo, garlic powder, and basil in a small bowl. Whisk together well.
3. Spread the mayo on the insides of each roll.
4. Top the inside of each sandwich with cheese, roasted bell peppers, ham, salami, capicollo, pepper rings, and another layer of cheese.
5. Close the sandwich, set on grill and close the lid for 3-5 min. Cook until warm and toasted.

BBQ Steak & Potato

True BBQ aficionados will be thrilled with this one. Tender, juicy steak go together with potatoes like soul food. Don't have time to sit down to a steak dinner? Enjoy this mouth watering combination for lunch!

Directions:

1. Preheat grill to medium-high heat.
2. Add room-temperature steak, onion and potato directly on the grill. Close lid and cook the steak until it starts to brown and remove meat to a plate.
3. Thinly slice the steak into slices while the onions and let the potatoes cook on the grill with the lid closed(15 min).
4. Butter the bread and sprinkle garlic salt and pepper. In between the bread, add the provolone, caramelized onions, green onion, potato, and steak slices and close the sandwich.
5. Set sandwich on the grill and press down the lid for 3-5 minutes, or until it is nice and toasted.

Ingredients:

1 Top sirloin steak
Provolone cheese
1 Potato (halved)
1 Green onion stalk
Butter
Garlic salt
Salt & pepper
Olive oil
Yellow onion (diced)
French bread

Korean Pulled Pork

It not hard to realize pulled pork just tastes absolutely amazing. In this sandwich, you get a newer and hipper — much more intense — Korean version of pulled pork to sink your teeth into. It takes a little longer to make, but is absolutely perfect on the weekends.

Ingredients:

1 3-4 pound Boston butt or pork butt

kosher salt and fresh ground black pepper

2 tbsps vegetable oil

1 medium size white onion, thinly sliced

2 Asian pears, stemmed, seeded and grated

5 cloves garlic, chopped

1 14.5 ounce can beef broth

1 cup brown sugar

3/4 cup soy sauce

3/4 cup rice vinegar (not seasoned)

1/4 cup Asian chili sauce

1/8 cup sesame oil

Sandwich rolls

Coleslaw, or kimchi

Directions:

To prepare the Korean Pulled Pork:

1. Preheat the oven to 300° F.
2. Season the pork butt liberally by sprinkling all sides with kosher salt and black pepper.
3. Heat vegetable oil in a large dutch oven over medium high heat and sear the pork until a nice crust forms (5 min per side). Remove from pan and set aside.
4. Add the onions, Asian pear and garlic and cook for about 3 minutes. Set the pork butt in the onion mixture.
5. Mix the beef broth, brown sugar, rice vinegar, Asian chili sauce and sesame oil in a large bowl or 4-cup measuring cup.
6. Pour over the pork and onions. Then cover the tray and cook in the oven for 4 hours or until the meat is tender and falling apart.
7. Transfer the pork to a large bowl and let cool. Shred using two forks.

To prepare the panini:

1. Place cooked meat in between two sandwich rolls and set on grill.
2. Close lid and grill panini for 2-3 min. Serve with coleslaw or kimchi.

Savory Brisket & Cheddar

The pungent meaty flavors of beef brisket will fill your kitchen as you prepare this. Sharp cheddar over perfectly tender brisket, this version is cooked with various spices and green leaves. The smell as it cooks will have you standing in the kitchen savoring it before it's even done.

Directions:

To prepare the corned beef:
1. Preheat the oven to 350° F.
2. Place the corn beef in a large glass baking tray and pour beer over top.
3. Mix together brown sugar, garlic, tomato paste, dijon mustard, soy sauce, balsamic vinegar, paprika and minced chipotle pepper in a bowl. Pour this mixture over the corn beef and add a bay leaf.
4. Cover and bake for 3.5 hours, or until the meat is tender and easy to shred with a fork.

To prepare the panini:
1. Preheat grill to medium-high heat.
2. Add the cooked beef to a sandwich roll with cheese, kale, and lemon juice.
3. Close the sandwich and set on grill. Close the lid to cook for 3-5 min.

Ingredients:

4 pounds corn beef brisket
2 cups stout beer
2 cloves garlic, minced or grated
1/2 cup brown sugar
1/3 cup tomato paste
1/3 cup balsamic vinegar
1/4 cup dijon mustard
1/4 cup soy sauce
1 teaspoon paprika
1 chipotle chile in adobo, minced
1 bay leaf
Cheddar cheese
1 cup kale

Kimchi Bulgogi Panini

Korean bulgogi truly is for meat lovers. Bulgogi is thinly sliced grilled and marinated beef with intense Asian flavors like sesame, soy, garlic, and ginger. This panini packs a flavor so complicatedly sweet and spicy, you will seriously kick yourself for not making this one sooner.

Ingredients:

1 lb tenderloin or rib eye
1/4 cup tamari (gluten-free soy sauce)
1 Tbsp sesame oil
2 large cloves garlic, finely minced
1/4 large onion, sliced thinly
1/4 Asian pear, grated (totally optional)
2-3 Tbsp agave nectar or honey
1 TB mirin
1/4 tsp black pepper
1 cup napa kimchi, sliced thinly
1 tsp gochujang (Korean red chili pepper paste)
1-2 tsp brown sugar or agave nectar

Directions:

1. Mix together tamari, sesame oil, minced garlic, agave nectar (or honey), mirin, and pepper in a bowl.
2. Add the thinly-sliced beef, sliced onions, and grated pear into a large ziploc bag. Next, add the marinade and shake well. Marinate overnight.
3. Preheat the grill to medium-high heat.
4. Add the beef and sauté until it's nicely browned.
5. Cook the sliced napa kimchi in a skillet over medium heat. Sauté until it becomes translucent and add brown sugar and gochujang paste. Mix well.
6. Carefully add the cooked beef and kimchi into a sub roll and close the sandwich.
7. Set the sandwich on the grill plates with some butter and close the lid to cook for 3-5 min, or until toasted and browned.

Seafood

Grilled Glazed Salmon

Spicy Chile Mahi Mahi

Greek Tuna Sun-Dried Tomato

**Fried Shrimp Po'Boy
with Jalapeno Lime Dressing**

Greek Tuna Sun Dried Tomato

Looking for a sandwich that is great for a healthy lunch? Gym-goers rejoice! This fantastic combination of tuna and sun dried tomato greek yogurt is a melt-in-your-mouth winner. Oh, and it's great for you.

Ingredients:

2 (9 by 10-inch) sheet frozen puff pastry, thawed and cut into 12 (3 by 5-inch) rectangles

2 (5 ounce) cans oil packed tuna

1/4 cup oil packed sun-dried tomatoes, chopped

1/2 cup pitted kalamata olives, halved

1 clove garlic, grated

2 teaspoons red wine vinegar

1 tbsp greek yogurt

1 teaspoon dried dill

1 teaspoon dried oregano

2 teaspoon dried parsley

2 cups baby spinach

1 avocado, pitted and sliced

1/2 cup feta cheese, crumbled

Directions:

1. Preheat the oven to 400° F and line two baking sheets with parchment paper.
2. Place the pastry rectangles on the baking sheets and prick holes in the pastries with a fork. Cover with another parchment paper and one more baking sheet before baking for 10-15 minutes.
3. While the pastries are baking, combine the tuna, sundried tomatoes, olives, and garlic in a large bowl. Mix together well.
4. Add red wine vinegar, dill, oregano, parsley, and greek yogurt. Mix thoroughly again.
5. Remove the golden pastries and top them with feta, spinach, layer of tuna mixture, and two slices of avocado.
6. Close the pastry with another pastry on top and set on grill.
7. Close the lid for 2-4 min. Cook until warm and toasted.

Spicy Chile Mahi Mahi

Take a walk on the wild side. You will have to prepare this spicy fish over the stove and get your hands dirty to make it right. It goes great in a golden-toasted panini.

Directions:

1. Preheat the grill to medium-high heat.
2. In a small saucepan, mix the sugar, lime juice and water. Bring to a boil over medium heat until mixture starts to thicken.
3. Stir in the minced red chile, garlic and pepper. Remove the saucepan from heat and whisk in fish sauce with 2 tbsp. of water. Set over medium heat again until sauce is smooth and sticky. Remove to a glass bowl and set aside.
4. Mix sesame oil and 1 tbsp thai red curry paste in a bowl. Brush this mixture over the mahi mahi and set on the grill to sear and close the lid (4-6 min).
5. Remove the fish and peel the skin away and chop into coarse chunks. Drizzle with the thick sauce you made first.
6. Assemble the sandwich by spreading mayo on the inside. Add the mahi mahi and top with soy sauce, chile oil, fresh cilantro, jalapenos, carrots, and cucumber slices.
7. Set sandwich on grill and close the lid for (2-4 min). Serve with more sauce.

Ingredients:

1 pound wild-caught, skin on, Mahi Mahi
3 tbsps sesame oil
1 tbsp thai red curry paste
1/2 cup granulated sugar
1 lime, juiced
1 tbsp water
1 red chile pepper
1 tbsp fish sauce
fresh pepper, taste
baguette
mayo

Grilled Glazed Salmon

Enjoy this delicious honey mustard glazed salmon with bacon and thinly-cut apple slices. A mix of sweet and savory, it's very different from how you normally eat salmon. You will want to try this on other fish too.

Ingredients:

1/4 cup(s) plus 2 tbsps Dijon mustard

1/4 cup(s) prepared horseradish, drained

2 tbsp(s) honey

4 6-ounce skinless salmon fillets

Vegetable oil, for rubbing

Salt and ground black pepper

4 kaiser rolls split, toasted and buttered

4 red lettuce leaves

8 thick bacon slices

1/2 Granny Smith apple, cut into 12 thin slices

Directions:

1. Preheat the grill to medium-high heat.
2. In a small bowl, mix the horseradish, honey, and mustard. Rub the salmon with oil and season with salt and pepper.
3. Add the salmon fillets to the grill and close the lid for (3-6 minutes), or until fully cooked.
4. Open lid and spoon some more horseradish glaze on the fillets. Close lid for 1 more minute.
5. Remove fillets and add bacon strips.
6. Spread horseradish glaze on the sub rolls. Add lettuce, crispy bacon, 2 slices of Granny Smith apple, and set a salmon fillet on top. Close the sandwich.
7. Set sandwich on grill and close the lid for (2-4 min), or until golden brown. Serve with more sauce.

Fried Shrimp Po'boy with Jalapeno-Lime Dressing

This is a classic New Orleans fried shrimp dish tossed in a luxurious jalapeno-lime dressing. You only get to enjoy shrimp once in a while, so you owe it to yourself to try this one. Crunch into some buttermilk-fried shrimp bites with a spicy sauce unlike anything you have ever tried.

Directions:

To prepare jalapeno-lime dressing:

1. Stir all the dressing ingredients together, except for the olive oil. Slowly whisk olive oil into the mixture until it combines well. (About 5 min of whisking should be enough)

To prepare fried shrimp:

1. Heat a large pan of oil to 375°.
2. Whisk the milk, buttermilk and sriracha sauce. Add shrimp and set in the fridge covered for at least 4 hours.
3. Meanwhile, mix the dry ingredients in a bowl — salt, paprika, cayenne, lemon pepper, garlic powder, cornstarch, flour, and cornmeal. Crack the two eggs in a separate bowl.
4. Dunk the shrimp in the eggs and then the dry mixture, shaking off excess powder. Place in the oil and fry for 2-3 minutes, or until golden brown. (When bubbles float to the top, they're ready).
5. Add the fried shrimp to a sandwich roll with your favorite toppings — cheese, onions, sauerkraut, whatever. It's also delicious with just crispy shrimp.
6. Set the sandwich on the grill and toast for 3-5 minutes, or until golden brown.

Ingredients:

½ cup milk
½ cup buttermilk
2 eggs
3 dashes of sriracha
1 cup AP flour
1 cup cornmeal
¾ cup cornstarch
2 tsp cajun seasoning
1 tsp salt
¼ tsp paprika
¼ tsp cayenne pepper
½ tsp lemon pepper
½ tsp garlic powder
2 pounds medium shrimp, peeled and deveined

Jalapeno-lime dressing:
½ tsp jalapeno juice
½ lime
½ cup olive oil
2 egg yolks
1 tsp dijon mustard
1 tsp white vinegar
½ tsp salt
¼ tsp black pepper
2 cloves garlic, minced

Juicy Lobster Rolls

Sink your claws into this delectable delight! Making fresh lobster takes some work, but it is worth it if you are willing to kill these critters yourself. Use store-bought prepared lobster

Ingredients:

3 1lb. lobsters
kosher salt
garlic mayo
½ cup lemon juice
additional lemon for serving
4 sub rolls

Directions:

1. Boil a large pot of water and add lobsters for 10-12 minutes. (It is more humane to kill them before boiling them alive).
2. Remove lobsters from pot and start cracking them open once cool enough to touch.
3. Separate the meat from the lobster into a large bowl. Chop into coarse pieces.
4. Spread the lobster meat into a single layer in the bowl and season with kosher salt. Add garlic mayo and lemon juice to taste. Mix well with a spatula.
5. Fill the sub rolls with the lobster meat and set on the grill.
6. Close the lid for 2-4 min. Cook until warm and toasted.

Veggie Paninis

Roasted Veggies with Pesto

Wild Mushroom Swiss Melt

Easy Spinach Artichoke Melt

Grilled Veggie Panini with Herbed Ricotta

Apple, Cheddar and Red Onion Melt

Easy Roasted Red Pepper & Basil

Easy Spinach & Artichoke Melt

Spinach and artichoke cheese dip is for everyone, not just vegetarians. Enjoy this classic dip remixed into a tasty panini with all-natural ingredients. Homemade is always better.

Ingredients:

2 tbsp. butter
1 clove garlic, minced or grated
1 tbsp flour
1/2 cup milk
1 ounce cream cheese
1/2 cup shredded mozzarella cheese
1/2 cup grated parmesan cheese
1/2 cup greek yogurt
1/2 teaspoon crushed red pepper flakes (optional)
1/2 teaspoon pepper
1/2 cup (about 5 ounces) frozen chopped spinach, thawed
1 (6.7 ounce) jar grilled artichoke hearts, chopped
4 slices thick sourdough or tuscan bread

Directions:

1. Melt butter in a skillet over medium heat. Throw in the minced garlic and cook for a few minutes.
2. Slowly add in flour and whisk till it becomes a nice paste. Pour in milk after two minutes and stir.
3. Preheat the grill to medium heat.
4. Next add cream cheese, mozzarella, parmesan and pepper. Keep stirring until the cheese melts completely, then add the greek yogurt, chopped artichokes and spinach. Stir well into a thick dip.
5. Spread the dip between each slice of bread and set the sandwich in the grill and close the lid. Cook for 3-5 minutes, or until the panini is golden brown.

Easy Roasted Red Pepper & Basil Melt

Roasted red peppers are absolutely delicious when topped with gooey cheese and juicy sundried tomatoes. Something happens to red peppers when they are roasted — they depart from the standard crisp and sharp garnish to something much more intensely sweet, juicy, and rich.

Directions:

1. Preheat the grill to medium-high heat.
2. Spread butter between each slice of bread and add roasted peppers, artichoke hearts, sundried tomatoes, basil, and mozzarella cheese. Close the sandwich.
3. Set the sandwich in the grill and close the lid. Cook for 3-5 minutes, or until the panini is golden brown.

Ingredients:

4 slices sourdough bread
8-10 Mozzarella Balls
1 cup roasted red peppers
4 Artichoke hearts
4 Sundried tomatoes
8 leaves fresh basil

Apple, Cheddar & Red Onion Melt

This sweet and savory panini absolutely hits the spot and is super easy to make. Bet you never thought to put apple slices in your sandwich with cheese and onions, but it adds an unbelievably new flavor sensation that is worth giving a shot.

Ingredients:

2 slices sourdough bread
1 apple, sliced
1 red onion, sliced
Sharp cheddar cheese slices
mayo

Directions:

1. Preheat the grill to medium-high heat.
2. Spread mayo between each slice of bread and add apple slices, red onions, and cheddar slices. Close the sandwich.
3. Set the sandwich in the grill and close the lid. Cook for 3-5 minutes, or until the panini is golden brown.

Roasted Veggies with Pesto

Roasted vegetables are an eclectic mix of powerful nutrients and wonderful tastes, sensations, and textures. Each vegetable blends with its neighbor perfectly to create a perfect marriage of flavor and essence.

Directions:

1. Preheat the grill to medium-high heat.
2. Spray the grill plates liberally with vegetable oil spray and add the chopped veggies. Close the lid and cook for 5-10 minutes, until veggies soften and have grill marks. Remove them to a plate when done.
3. Spread pesto between each slice of bread and add veggies and mozzarella and feta.
4. Set the sandwich in the grill and close the lid. Cook for 3-5 minutes, or until the panini is golden brown.

Ingredients:

3 bell peppers, chopped

1 onion, chopped

8 oz. mushrooms, chopped

Asparagus, chopped

Shredded mozzarella

Crumbled feta

Pesto

Italian bread

Olive oil

Kosher salt

Wild Mushroom Swiss Melt

Cooking wild mushrooms releases more flavor and makes them much more pleasant to enjoy in a meal. Garnished with fresh herbs and spices, this wild mushroom mix pairs wonderfully with the nutty and sweet flavor of Swiss cheese.

Ingredients:

1 tbsp extra virgin olive oil
1 tbsp unsalted butter
1/4 cup thinly sliced shallots
2 teaspoons minced garlic
2-1/2 cups sliced wild
    mushrooms, such as shiitake,
    chanterelle or porcini
1 tbsp balsamic vinegar
1 tbsp chopped fresh parsley
Coarse salt and black pepper
Swiss cheese
4 slices sourdough bread

Directions:

1. Preheat the grill to medium-high heat.
2. Grab a skillet and heat a mixture of olive oil and butter over medium heat for 2 minutes. Add shallots and garlic, cooking them for a minute. Stir well.
3. Throw in the wild mushroom mix and cook until tender, stirring well. Add balsamic vinegar, parsley, and salt and pepper.
4. Spread butter between each slice of bread, and add mushrooms and top with swiss cheese.
5. Set the sandwich in the grill and close the lid. Cook for 3-5 minutes, or until the panini is golden brown.

Fried Green Tomato Delight

Generally considered unripe tomatoes, some enjoy them for their tart flavor. There are also ripe tomatoes that are naturally green, and both provide a unique flavor when fried. Fried green tomatoes go very well with salty and spicy flavors.

Directions:

1. Set the egg mixture, cornmeal, and flour in 3 separate bowls. Season the cornmeal liberally with salt and pepper in a bowl.
2. Dip the tomato slices in the flour, then in the egg mixture, and then in the cornmeal. Do this for the rest of the tomato slices and set them aside.
3. Preheat the grill to medium-high heat.
4. In a large skillet, heat oil until it's nice and hot. Add the tomato slices and cook over medium-high heat, flipping once for 2.5 min per side. Drain the slices on a paper towel.
5. Spread mayo between each slice of bread, add the tomato slices and arugula, then set the sandwich in the grill and close the lid. Cook for 3-5 minutes, or until the panini is golden brown.

Ingredients:

1/2 cup(s) all-purpose flour
1 large egg beaten with 1 tbsp of water
1/2 cup(s) yellow cornmeal
Salt and freshly ground pepper
1 pound(s) unripe green tomatoes or large tomatillos, cut into 1/2-inch slices
Canola oil
4 thick-cut slices of whole wheat or multigrain bread, toasted
Mayo
baby arugula

Grilled Veggie Panini with Herb Ricotta

Another grilled veggie sensation for you to try. But this recipe showcases summer and spring grilled vegetables with the intense flavor of herbed ricotta cheese. Enjoy the juicy and creamy texture of this veggie mix drizzled in flavorful herbs and soft cheese.

Ingredients:

1 cup ricotta cheese
1 tbsp each of fresh basil, chives and parsley, chopped
1 clove garlic, minced
1 tbsp extra virgin olive oil plus more for drizzling
kosher salt and freshly ground black pepper
1 portobello mushroom
1 medium zucchini, sliced lengthwise
1 medium yellow squash, sliced lengthwise
1/2 medium eggplant, sliced into rounds
1/2 red onion, peeled and sliced into rounds
1/2 red bell pepper, seeded and sliced in half or quarters
2 teaspoons dried oregano
1 loaf ciabatta bread or other soft bread sliced into 6-inch sections and cut in half
1/2 cup arugula leaves
Balsamic vinegar

Directions:

1. Preheat the grill to medium-high heat.
2. Grab a bowl and throw in the ricotta cheese, fresh herbs, garlic clove, tbsp. of extra virgin olive oil, salt and pepper. Mix well until consistency is smooth.
3. Spray the grill plates with vegetable oil spray and add the sliced veggies. Close the lid and cook for 5-10 minutes, until veggies soften and have grill marks. Remove them to a plate when done.
4. Spread the herb ricotta between each slice of bread and add veggies and arugula. Splash a little balsamic vinegar over the arugula.
5. Set the sandwich in the grill and close the lid. Cook for 3-5 minutes, or until the panini is golden brown.

Panini with Lemon-Basil Pesto

Lemon-basil pesto is an incredibly simple, yet powerful taste.

Directions:

To make basil-lemon pesto:

1. Combine the garlic, pine nuts, basil, and salt in a blender and mix until consistency is smooth. Add oil and lemon juice and mix again.

To make panini:

1. Preheat the grill to medium-high heat.
2. Add the chopped bell peppers, onions, and squash to the grill for 7-10 min, or until they are well-done. Remove them to a plate.
3. Spread the lemon-basil pesto on the bread slices and drizzle lightly with vinegar.
4. Add the tomatoes, bell peppers, onions, squash, and avocado slices to each slice of bread evenly. Sprinkle with salt and pepper.
5. Set the sandwich in the grill and close the lid. Cook for 3-5 minutes, or until the panini is golden brown.

Ingredients:

2 medium-size roasted red bell peppers, cut lengthwise into slices

3 zucchini squash, sliced and roasted or grilled

1 medium-size red onion, sliced

1 or 2 medium-size tomatoes, sliced

1 ripe avocado, peeled and sliced

4 large slices Italian bread, such as ciabatta

2 tbsp balsamic vinegar

salt and pepper

Olive oil, for brushing

2 cups loosely packed fresh basil leaves

2 whole garlic cloves, peeled

1/4 cup pine nuts

salt, to taste

2 tbsps olive oil

1 to 2 teaspoons fresh lemon juice

BREAKFASTS

Sharp & Sweet Egg Sandwich

Roasted Red Pepper Breakfast Panini

Fully-Loaded Spanish Omelette

Ridiculously Simple Hash Browns

Egg & Biscuit Big Daddy

Ultimate Breakfast Griddle

Ridiculously Simple Hash Browns

If you're like most people, you crave crispy hash browns as a side with your eggs and sausage in the morning. Keep a zip loc bag with grated potatoes stashed in the fridge to quickly throw them in the grill in the morning.

Directions:

1. Start with a cold grill.
2. Grate the potatoes directly onto the grill plates in 4 big piles. Gently shape the mounds into flat "patties".
3. Drizzle each mound with a bit of the butter, then sprinkle with salt and pepper.
4. Close the grill and turn on. Cook until crispy and browned, about 6 to 7 minutes. Serve hot and fresh.

Ingredients:

2 medium russet potatoes, peeled
1 tbsp butter, melted
Salt and ground black pepper, to taste
Start with a cold panini press or countertop grill.

The Ultimate Breakfast Griddle

Are you tired of feeling sluggish at work? Put that energy shot down and feed your body a nutritious breakfast instead. You can make a tasty protein-packed griddle that will give you the boost of energy you crave in the mornings. Opt for fresher and higher-quality ingredients to increase the energy surge.

Ingredients:

4 frozen whole wheat waffles, toasted

3-4 eggs

Salt and pepper, to taste

1 tbsp butter

2 cooked sausage patties

Directions:

1. Preheat the grill to medium.
2. Crack the eggs into a beaker. Add butter, salt, and pepper.
3. Scramble the mixture and pour the eggs onto the grill.
4. Crumble the sausage patties into the eggs or let them cook as patties if you prefer.
5. Add cheese as the eggs are just about done cooking.
6. Assemble sandwiches and top with butter and syrup. To make these for "on-the-go", spread a little butter and jelly inside the waffles before putting the sandwich together.

Fully-Loaded Spanish Omelette

Loaded with protein and lacking in all those carbs, you're sure to enjoy this tasty omelette. The protein will keep you going for hours. Making a simple omelette has never been easier with your indoor grill.

Directions:

1. Preheat the grill to medium.
2. Set the bacon strips over the grill plates.
3. Cook the bacon until crispy and brown (2-3 min).
4. Remove the bacon, but leave the fat.
5. Throw in the spinach, onions and tomatoes.
6. Pour the eggs over the spinach and close the lid.
7. After 1-2 min (or more depending on how many eggs you use), remove the omelette from the grill.
8. Roll into a cigar or cut into strips to serve with the bacon on the side.

Ingredients:

2 slices bacon
1 -ounce fresh spinach
2 eggs
½ cup chopped onions
½ cup diced tomatoes

Sharp and Sweet Egg Sandwich

Egg sandwiches are the perfect breakfast meal. This egg sandwich is guaranteed to not only get you out of bed, but help you start the day the right way. It has just a hint of sweetness to it to help get your day off to a good start.

Ingredients:

2 slices bacon

2 large eggs

2 slices sandwich bread

1 slice sharp cheddar cheese

2 tbsp strawberry jam

Directions:

1. Cook the bacon in a large pan over medium-high heat until it gets nice and crispy (3-5 min). Transfer the bacon to a paper towel-lined plate.
2. Pour out most of the bacon grease from the pan, but leave about 2 tbsps worth in the pan.
3. Preheat the grill.
4. Crack the eggs into the grease in the pan. Sprinkle black pepper over the eggs and fry them until the whites are fully cooked and the yolks are just barely set.
5. Spread the jam on the top slice of the bread and the cheese on the bottom. Add the cooked eggs and bacon and close the sandwich.
6. Press down the sandwich with the lid and grill for 3-5 min, or until lightly toasted.

Egg & Waffle Big Daddy

Don't be tired when you're heading off to work! This is a breakfast which has a boost of protein in it to give you the energy you need to be awesome. So put down that extra cup of coffee and eat this instead.

Directions:

1. Preheat the grill to medium.
2. Crack the eggs into a beaker. Add butter, salt, and pepper.
3. Scramble the mixture and pour the eggs onto the grill.
4. Crumble the sausage patties into the eggs or let them cook as patties if you prefer.
5. Add cheese as the eggs are just about done cooking.
6. Assemble sandwiches and top with butter and syrup. To make these for "on-the-go", spread a little butter and jelly inside the waffles before putting the sandwich together.

Ingredients:

4 frozen whole wheat waffles, toasted
3-4 eggs
Salt and pepper, to taste
1 tbsp butter
2 cooked sausage patties

Eggs and Bacon Breakfast Panini

Are you a person who prefers a classic breakfast? We bring you a panini that's simple and to the point. It has all the staples of your average breakfast for those of you on the go.

Ingredients:

3 bacon slices, thick-cut
2 large eggs
2 tsp fresh tarragon
2 oz. cheddar cheese
1 English muffins, or whole-
    wheat bread
2 tbsp unsalted butter

Directions:

1. Preheat the grill to medium-high heat.
2. Add bacon and cook until crispy (5–8 minutes). Transfer to paper towels to drain and discard the bacon drippings.
3. Spread both sides of the English muffins with the remaining tbsp of butter. Slice the muffins in half and set face down in the grill. Close the lid and cook until lightly toasted (1–2 minutes).
4. While the muffins are toasting, grab a frying pan and melt a little butter. Next, crack the eggs into the pan. Cook over medium heat until the whites are set but the yolks are still runny (3–4 minutes).
5. Sprinkle with the tarragon and season with salt and pepper. Flip the eggs and cook until the yolks are softly set (1 min).
6. Add cheese to the bottom half of each muffin, the eggs, and bacon slices. Divide the remaining cheese on top. Cover with the muffin tops, cut sides down, and press gently.
7. Close the top plate and cook until the muffins are golden and toasted and the cheese is melted (4–5 minutes). Serve.

Roasted Red Pepper Breakfast Panini

When it comes to breakfast you need to be prepared for anything. If you're looking for a way to wake up quick, fast, and have a boost of energy this panini is your best option.

Directions:

1. Preheat the grill to medium-high heat.
2. Scramble eggs and milk together.
3. Cook the eggs thoroughly (in a pan or the grill) and add roasted red peppers.
4. Mix the butter and herbs together in a small bowl. Spread on outside of sourdough bread.
5. Put cooked eggs on bread and place in the panini.
6. Close the lid and toast sandwich until golden brown (3-5 min).

Ingredients:

Sourdough bread
3 eggs, scrambled
1 tbsp milk
½ cup roasted red peppers
½ tbsp Italian seasoning
1.5 tbsp butter, softened

Bacon-Stuffed Pancake Surprise

Who would have thought you could wake up to such a powerful breakfast in the morning? These pancakes are perfect on the weekends. Just the tantalizing aroma of bacon, pancakes and syrup will have the whole family jumping out of bed and to the dining table. The surprise is all in the bacon, in case you didn't get that yet.

Ingredients:

6 slices of bacon
1 cup prepared pancake batter
(from a mix or from scratch)
softened butter
maple syrup

Directions:

1. Preheat the griddler to medium-high.
2. Throw the bacon on until it's crisp. Remove and place on paper towel.
3. Wipe the griddle gently with paper towels to remove the grease. Leave a little on to let the pancakes cook.
4. Throw the bacon back on the grill, but spaced apart an inch or two.
5. Slowly pour the batter over the bacon strips.
6. Flip the pancake when browned and remove once both sides are done.

Triple Attack Breakfast Monster

Meat. Eggs. Cheese. Waffles and syrup. What more do you need to know? Satisfy all the sensations from meaty to sweet and please your palate before rushing off to work. Obviously, the fresher ingredients you use, the healthier and tastier this monster will be. But you already knew that, you smarty-pants.

Directions:

1. Preheat the grill to medium.
2. Pop the waffles in toaster (or make homemade ones)
3. Pour the shredded cheese over the meat in a bowl and mix well.
4. Roll the sausage into a large ball.
5. Flatten into a nice thick patty.
6. Make a hole in the center of the patty with a small cup or bowl
7. Let the meat brown evenly and then crack an egg into the hole in the center. The sausage should be just about done as you let the egg cook.
8. Make sure both sides are cooking evenly.
9. Remove the sausage and throw it in between two hot-and-ready waffles.

Ingredients:

½ lb sausage
½ cup shredded cheese
1 egg
Waffles (homemade or frozen)
Syrup (optional)

Ultimate Quesadillas

Twisted Pepperoni Pizza

Steak & Caramelized Onion

Spicy Chipotle Chicken

Cheesy Broccoli Red Onion

Spicy Picante Spinach

Picante Spinach Quesadillas

Don't be fooled by the name, its not that spicy. Loaded with spinach and cheese, this one is sure to please anyone. It's a sneaky way to load your meals with healthy spinach.

Directions:

1. Heat ¼ cup of water in a large skillet over medium heat.
2. Throw in the spinach, sprinkle with salt, and cover for about 5 min. Stir well until spinach is soft and tender.
3. Drain the water out thoroughly, until spinach is just almost dry.
4. Preheat the grill to medium-low heat.
5. Place 1-2 tortillas on the warm grill and spread a thin layer of cheese over the surface.
6. Add a layer of spinach leaves evenly over the cheese.
7. When cheese is starting to melt, add a tbsp of salsa.
8. If desired, add the chipotle chicken mixture over half the tortilla.
9. To seal the quesadilla, fold the side of the tortilla that does not have salsa on it over the top.
10. Close the lid and let it cook for 4-6 min, or until the tortilla is crispy.

Ingredients:

6 oz. baby spinach
pinch of kosher salt
8 small or 4 large tortillas
8 oz. pepper jack cheese, grated
fresh spicy salsa or pico de gallo
diced or shredded cooked
    chicken, optional

Twisted Pepperoni Pizza Quesadilla

You'll be kicking yourself for not thinking of this yourself. A ridiculously welcome twist on the classic pepperoni pizza. And it's easier to hold and eat so it won't leave your hands feeling greasy.

Ingredients:

4 flour tortillas
4 ounces of shredded mozzarella
  cheese
3 ounces sliced pepperoni
1 (16-ounce) jar of pizza sauce
butter for pan

Directions:

1. Preheat the grill to medium-high heat.
2. Add a little butter and then the pepperoni until they start becoming crispy (3-4 min).
3. Remove them and place them on a paper towel to drain.
4. Brush each tortilla with a thin layer of pizza sauce.
5. Place the tortilla on the grill and sprinkle cheese on top of the sauce
6. Top with the pepperoni and other toppings, if desired. Sprinkle with another layer of cheese if you add more toppings.
7. Close the lid for 4-6 min, or until the tortilla is crispy.
8. Slice into quarters and serve with a little bowl of warm pizza sauce for dipping.

Cheesy Broccoli Red Onion Quesadilla

You know you should be eating more broccoli, but you're probably not. Tell you what, try this quesadilla and tell me you don't love it. I dare you. Cheese and onions make anything taste great — even broccoli.

Directions:

Making the broccoli filling:

1. Preheat the grill to medium-high heat.
2. Microwave the bag of frozen broccoli as per the instructions on the bag. Or bring a pot of water to a boil and add the broccoli crowns for four minutes and remove.
3. Rinse with cold water and pat them dry with a paper towel.
4. Chop them into small little florets for easier cooking.
5. Spoon some butter over the grill plates and add the red onions.
6. Cook for 4-5 min, or until they start to sear on the edges.
7. Now add the sliced broccoli.
8. Cook, stirring, until broccoli starts to sear as well (roughly 3 min).
9. Remove from the grill and stir in the cilantro, season with salt and pepper.

To make the quesadillas:

1. Drain the water out thoroughly, until spinach is just almost dry.
2. Preheat the grill to medium-low heat.
3. Place 1-2 tortillas on the warm grill and spread a thin layer of cheese over the surface.
4. Add the broccoli filling evenly over the cheese.
5. When cheese is starting to melt, add a tbsp of salsa.
6. To seal the quesadilla, fold the side of the tortilla that does not have salsa on it over the top.
7. Close the lid and let it cook for 4-6 min, or until the tortilla is crispy.

Ingredients:

1 large broccoli crown, about 1/2 pound
1 tbsp extra virgin olive oil
1 medium red onion, chopped
1 tbsp cilantro, chopped
Salt and freshly ground pepper
4 corn tortillas
½ cup grated cheddar or mixed cheeses
Salsa for serving (optional)

Steak and Caramelized Onion Quesadilla

Steak and caramelized onions really do go together well....really well. With a dash of barbecue sauce, this is sure to be a summer favorite to share amongst friends. Plus, its a great way to get rid of all that extra steak.

Ingredients:

½ of a steak
Havarti cheese
Thyme
Onions
Barbecue sauce
Butter
1 tortilla
Garden vegetable cream cheese
Tomato based pizza/pasta sauce

Directions:

To prepare the steak:

1. Generously sprinkle salt and pepper over the steak.
2. Preheat the grill to medium-high heat.
3. Add olive oil after a minute, then the steak.
4. Close the lid and let the steak cook to your preferred "doneness". For medium, cook it until your meat thermometer reads 137°F.
5. Remove the steak when its done and set it on a cutting board for 5-10 min.
6. Slice it into thin slices.

To make the quesadilla:

1. Preheat the grill to medium heat
2. Add butter and sauté the onions for 3-5 min. Remove when done.
3. Melt some butter in your pan until it's sizzling and then place a tortilla on the hot grill.
4. Spread cream cheese on one half and pasta sauce on the other half.
5. Add cheese on one side, then your steak slices, onions, and a pinch of thyme.
6. Close the lid and cook this for about 3-5 min, or until the quesadilla is golden and crispy on both sides. Serve with the barbecue sauce.

Traditional Chipotle Chicken

It takes a little longer to prepare, but is worth the trouble. It's sure to tantalize and sizzle your tongue with its south of the border taste.

Directions:

Preparing the chipotle chicken:

1. Preheat a skillet to medium-high heat.
2. Spoon some oil in and add the onion, sprinkle with salt, and sauté for about 3 min.
3. Add the garlic and sauté until the onions start to brown (roughly 2 min).
4. Mix in the chipotle chiles and the tomatoes.
5. Cook until most of the liquid from the tomatoes has evaporated and the mixture begins to thicken, stirring often, about 20 minutes.
6. Stir in the green onions and honey slowly.
7. Finally, add the chicken and cook until the chicken is fully cooked.

Making the quesadillas:

1. Preheat the grill to medium-low heat.
2. Place 2 tortillas on the hot grill for about 2 min and then flip them over.
3. Sprinkle 1/2 cup of cheese over the bottom halves of the tortillas and add chicken mixture.
4. Add a little more cheese and top with avocado slices.
5. Fold the tortillas over to cover the fillings and make a crescent shape.
6. Cook until the tortillas are crisp and golden and the cheese has melted (3 min)
7. Sprinkle the cilantro in the quesadilla by opening them just a little. Serve with lime wedges and sour cream.

Ingredients:

Chipotle Chicken:

3 tbsps olive oil

1 red onion, finely chopped (about 1 1/2 cups)

Kosher salt and freshly ground black pepper

3 garlic cloves, finely chopped

5 chipotle chilies in adobo sauce, finely chopped

3 vine-ripened tomatoes (about 1 1/4 lbs. total), diced

3 green onions, thinly sliced

1 tbsp honey

3 cups coarsely shredded roasted chicken breast

Quesadillas:

Four 10-inch-diameter flour tortillas

3 cups shredded white cheddar cheese (about 12 ounces)

2 avocados, peeled, pitted, sliced

1/2 cup fresh cilantro leaves

1/3 cup sour cream

4 lime wedges

ULTIMATE DESSERTS

Warm Nutella Banana Sandwich

Decadent Blueberry Mozzarella

S'more Panini

Caramel Apple Cream
Cheese Quesadilla

Easy Pillsbury Cinnabon Rolls

Easy Pillsbury Cinnabon Rolls

This one is a no-brainer. No preparation involved at all! Just pop out a can of Pillsbury Cinnabon rolls and throw them on the grill. They come out toasted and delicious, especially with frosting after they're done.

Directions:

1. Butter both sides of the Cinnabon Cinnamon Rolls and set aside.
2. Preheat the grill to medium-high heat.
3. Place the rolls on the warm grill, giving as much space between each roll as possible.
4. Press the lid down gently to flatten the rolls.
5. Let them cook for 3-4 min, or until browned well.
6. Spread the icing included in the package over them. Enjoy hot and fresh.

Ingredients:

1 can of Pillsbury Cinnabon Cinnamon Rolls, opened

Warm Nutella Banana Sandwich

Anybody who says they don't love Nutella is a liar! Now you can use that sweet sweet spread to make a warm and toasty sandwich with mashed bananas. It's surprisingly simple. Once you try warm Nutella on toasted bread, you'll never want to go back. Warning: friends who see you lighting a spoonful of Nutella might give you looks!

Add strawberries to this sandwich to give it an even better twist.

Ingredients:

1 ripe banana, sliced
4 slices whole-wheat bread
Nutella spread
4 tbsp unsalted butter, softened
1 tbsp confectioners' sugar
  (optional)

Directions:

1. Set the bananas in a bowl and mash until they reach a smooth consistency.
2. Spread the Nutella to your liking on 2 slices of bread
3. Now spread the mashed banana over the other 2 slices and combine the slices to make 2 sandwiches.
4. Preheat the grill to medium-low.
5. Spoon a tbsp of butter over the top and bottom of each sandwich and place on the warm grill.
6. Grill until golden brown (about 3-5 min).
7. Remove from the grill and sprinkle with the confectioners' sugar, if desired. Eat while its hot and fresh.

Caramel Apple Cream Cheese Quesadilla

Homemade caramel sauce tastes so much better, but if you must use store-bought, then try to get one that isn't full of chemicals posing as caramel. The cream cheese in this quesadilla goes really well with caramel apples (which are already great on their own).

Directions:

Preparing the caramel sauce:
1. Grab a small saucepan and add the caramels and heavy cream over low-medium heat. (You could also use a microwave to melt the caramels and cream together, but you would have to stop and stir every minute or so.)
2. It is important that you stir constantly and let the caramels melt completely.
3. Once melted, turn off the stove and let the caramel sit in the pan until ready to use.

Making the quesadillas:
1. Preheat the grill to medium-low heat and add butter.
2. Place a tortilla on the grill and top with 1-2 ounces of cream cheese.
3. Top the cream cheese with an even layer of thinly sliced apples.
4. Cover the open tortilla with another one to seal the quesadilla. Press down to make them tight.
5. Close the lid and let the quesadilla cook until the cheese begins to melt (about 3 min).
6. Check on the tortilla every min or so to make sure the bottom is browning.
7. When golden and crispy, remove the quesadilla and place on a large cutting board.
8. Cut into 4 equal pieces and drizzle caramel sauce over the quesadillas. Serve hot and fresh.

Ingredients:

Simple Caramel Sauce:
14 Werther's Original® Baking Caramels, unwrapped
1 tbsp heavy cream, half-and-half, or full fat milk
Quesadilla:
butter or oil, for the pan
4 whole wheat tortillas
4-6 ounces cream cheese
1 small apple, thinly sliced

Crunchy Peanut Butter & Jelly Sandwich

Now here's a weird twist on a classic sandwich. Even your 5-year old niece can make a peanut butter jelly sandwich. But can she toast it with crushed cornflakes and make it warm and gooey inside?

Didn't think so.

Ingredients:

4 slices of bread
1 egg
A dash of milk
1.5 cup cornflakes
Peanut butter
Jelly or Jam
Butter to grease the pan

Directions:

1. Pour cornflakes into bowl and crush them with your hands or a large spoon.
2. Crack an egg with a dash of milk in a separate bowl and beat well.
3. Preheat the grill to medium-low heat.
4. Spread the jelly on one slice of bread and peanut butter on the other slice.
5. Combine them to make a regular peanut butter jelly sandwich.
6. Dip the sandwich in the egg mixture making sure to cover both sides.
7. Now dunk them in the cornflake crumbs.
8. Spoon some butter onto the hot grill and add the sandwich and close the lid.
9. Once the sandwich is golden brown, remove and serve hot and fresh.

S'more Panini

Miss those days when you could sit around campfire eating s'mores? Well, no longer do you have to worry about those days gone by! Now you can have our version of s'mores whenever the desire hits you.

Directions:

1. Preheat grill to medium-high heat.
2. Spread a generous portion of Nutella on both slices of bread.
3. Sprinkle the chopped nuts over one slice and top with marshmallows. Combine them to make a sandwich.
4. Spoon some butter onto the hot grill and add the sandwich and close the lid.
5. Once the sandwich is golden brown, remove and serve hot and fresh (3-5 min).

Ingredients:

1 jar of Nutella
2 large marshmallows cut in half
2 thin slices sourdough
1 oz chopped nuts

Decadent Blueberry Mozzarella

This is the most unusual and strangely delicious tasting sensation you will ever try. Europeans love eating fruits with cheese, but this is a uniquely American taste. Warm and gooey mozzarella cheese swirling with sweet and juicy blueberry sauce — your mouth will thank you.

Ingredients:

2 slices sourdough bread
½ ball of fresh mozzarella, sliced
1.5 oz. cream cheese (or butter)
A few tbsps of blueberry balsamic
    sauce
A handful of fresh basil leaves
For the blueberry sauce:
5 oz blueberries
2 tsps honey
1 tbsp balsamic vinegar
2 tsps lemon juice
1 tsp black pepper

Directions:

To make easy blueberry sauce:
1. Mix all the ingredients in a saucepan over medium heat for 15 minutes. Stir well and remove when sauce thickens.

To make the panini:
1. Preheat grill to medium heat.
2. Spread cream cheese on one slice of bread and cover with slices of mozzarella.
3. Set the basil leaves over cheese and spoon blueberry sauce on top.
4. Brush a little oil on the outside of the panini, set on the grill, and close the lid.
5. Grill until the mozzarella is melted and the bread is golden brown.

Chocolate and Brie

Are you a chocolate lover? Awesome! Here's an amazing way to get your chocolate fix with a new, exciting twist to it. We bring you the eclectic taste of creamy and flavorful brie cheese entangled with the classic sweet chocolatey taste.

Directions:

1. Preheat grill to medium-high heat.
2. Spread the cheese slices on two pieces of bread. Top each slice with chocolate.
3. Combine the pieces to make sandwiches and brush the outside with melted butter.
4. Set sandwich on the grill and close the lid.
5. Grill until the cheese is melted and the bread is golden brown.

Ingredients:

4 slices crunchy sourdough bread
4 oz. Brie cheese, cut into slices
2 oz. milk chocolate
2 tbsps unsalted butter, melted

3-Minute Grilled Snickers

We all know snickers taste great on their own. Have you ever tried one perfectly melted into a sandwich with some peanut butter? Both kids and adults will go nuts over this one.

Ingredients:

2 slices bread

SNICKERS bar (large or minis), chopped

2 tbsp peanut butter

2 tbsps unsalted butter, melted

Directions:

1. Preheat grill to medium-high heat.
2. Spread peanut butter on two slices of bread
3. Add the Snickers pieces and combine the pieces to make sandwiches
4. Brush the outside with melted butter set sandwich on the grill.
5. Close the lid and grill until the chocolate is melted and the bread is golden brown.

QUICK MEALS TO BEAT THE HUNGER

Most of us don't have the time to plan or prepare our meals, or we're just too lazy and make excuses. Whatever your reason for grabbing fast food or eating out excessively, you can easily change the quality of your home-cooked meals by having your ingredients chopped and ready to go in the fridge.

Most of the meals in this cookbook are very filling on their own, but if you're hosting a party or friends come over spontaneously, these ultimate sides are sure to please everyone. And if you're just really hungry....well, mix and match paninis and quesadillas with these sides as you like.

Some of them might require a little preparation outside of the grill, but if you chop and stash ingredients ahead, it won't take very long to get these quick meals ready.

ULTIMATE SIDES

Broccoli with Lemon Crumbs

Smashed Potatoes with Gorgonzola & Sage

Lemon-Glazed Veggies with Pasta

Perfectly Roasted Sweet Potato Wedges

Hearty Red Bell Pepper & Green Bean Toss

Honey-Glazed Baby Carrots

Creamed Corn

Garlic Mint Peas

Grilled Okra and Tomatoes

No one knows what to do with okra. They're weird and hard to incorporate into many dishes. But as a side? Hallelujah! Now we're talkin'.

Directions:

1. Preheat grill to medium-high heat.
2. In a large bowl, combine all the ingredients.
3. Place mixture on cooking grate, and grill, covered with grill lid, over medium-high heat (350° to 400°). Grill tomatoes 3 minutes or just until they get grill marks.
4. Turn okra, and grill, covered with grill lid, 2 to 3 more minutes or until tender.
5. Transfer okra and tomatoes to a serving dish, and sprinkle with basil. Serve immediately.

Ingredients:

1 pound fresh okra, trimmed
1 pt. cherry tomatoes
2 tbsps olive oil
1/2 teaspoon salt
1/2 teaspoon pepper
2 tbsps chopped fresh basil

Smashed Potatoes with Gorgonzola and Sage

This side does not require using the grill, but is too delicious of a side to leave out. It pairs really well with just about any meat, panini, or quesadilla. If you don't have gorgonzola at home, try it with cheddar for an equally unique flavor.

Ingredients:

2 pounds unpeeled Yukon gold potatoes

1 1/2 tbsps butter

1/2 cup 1% low-fat milk

1/2 teaspoon kosher salt

1/2 teaspoon freshly ground black pepper

1/4 cup crumbled Gorgonzola or other blue cheese

1 tbsp chopped fresh sage

Directions:

1. Drop the potatoes in a saucepan filled with water (the potatoes should be fully submerged)
2. Bring to a boil for 20 minutes or until the potatoes are tender
3. Drain the water. Careful, the potatoes will be very hot!
4. Place the potatoes in a large bowl and mix in butter, milk, salt, and pepper.
5. Mash coarsely with a potato masher (or use the pulse setting in a blender)
6. Add Gorgonzola and chopped fresh sage.

Mixed Corn Succotash

This one requires a little preparation outside of the grill...about 2-3 minute's worth. If you're bored of salads with your meat, give this one a shot. You won't regret it.

Directions:

1. To blanch the fava beans, drop them in a pot of lightly salted boiling water for about 2 minutes
2. Drain and rinse the beans under cold water to stop the cooking.
3. Peel off and discard the green skins; set the beans side.
4. Preheat the grill to medium-high heat.
5. Spoon a little oil on the grill plate and add the corn, onion, garlic, and salt and cook.
6. Using a fork or spoon, stir the vegetables until they are slightly charred and golden (5-7 min).
7. Lastly, add the bell pepper and beans and cook an additional 2 minutes.
8. Remove from heat, add the scallions, and toss well. Serve warm or at room temperature.

Ingredients:

1 pound fresh fava beans, shelled (1 cup)
2 tbsps olive oil
4 cups fresh corn kernels, cut from 4 ears of corn
1 small onion, finely diced
2 small garlic cloves, minced
1 teaspoon kosher salt
1/2 red pepper, thinly sliced
1 scallion, thinly sliced

Lemon-Glazed Veggies with Pasta

Full disclosure: this dish does not use the grill at all. But it's so easy to make and pairs well with chicken and turkey. It doesn't take very long to make either!

Ingredients:

1/2 (16-oz.) package rigatoni pasta

1 small onion, chopped

2 tbsps olive oil

3/4 cup chicken broth

2 teaspoons lemon zest

2 tbsps fresh lemon juice

1 cup fresh snow peas

1 cup matchstick carrots

2 tbsps chopped fresh basil

2 tbsps butter

1/2 teaspoon chopped fresh thyme

3/4 teaspoon salt

1/4 teaspoon freshly ground pepper

Directions:

1. Prepare pasta according to packageDirections.
2. In a skillet, spoon a little oil or butter over medium-heat.
3. Sauté the onions for 3-5 min, or until slightly browned.
4. Reduce heat to medium and stir in chicken broth, lemon zest, lemon juice, snow peas and carrots.
5. Bring to a boil and cook for 3-4 minutes or until most of the liquid evaporates.
6. Stir in hot cooked pasta, basil, butter, and thyme.
7. Cook, stirring occasionally, for 2-4 min. Season with salt and pepper.

Garlic and Mint Peas

This recipe requires some boiling before using the grill. You might have already noticed that the shape of the griddler does not contain water very well. Who would have thought garlic and mint goes really well together?

Directions:

1. Boil a large saucepan of water and add the snap peas for 2-3 minutes.
2. Drain and rinse them under running cold water.
3. Set the griddler to 350 degrees and cook the garlic halves in the oil until golden.
4. Remove and discard the garlic (unless you finely chopped them, they will be too strong to use with the peas)
5. Finally, add the sugar snap peas and fresh or thawed peas and cook until tender (3-5 min). Stirring them with a wooden spoon ensures one side doesn't get burned
6. Turn off the heat and add the mint, sugar, and salt.

Ingredients:

1 pound sugar snap peas (2 cups)
2 cloves garlic, halved
1 tbsp canola oil
2 cups fresh or thawed frozen peas
1/4 cup fresh mint leaves, chopped, or 1 tbsp dried mint
1/2 teaspoon sugar
1/2 teaspoon salt

Broccoli with Lemon Crumbs

Another quick and tasty way to get more broccoli in your diet. Extra emphasis on the quick and tasty! You can freeze the lemon crumbs for 2-3 days before they start going bad.

Ingredients:

2 slices whole-wheat bread

2 tbsps butter

1 lemon

Olive oil

1/2 teaspoon kosher salt

Freshly ground black pepper

2 12-ounce bags broccoli florets, or

1 large bunch broccoli, cut into florets

Directions:

1. Making the lemon crumbs:
2. Throw the bread in a food processor or blender to make bread crumbs.
3. Melt the butter in either a small skillet or on the grill.
4. Add the bread crumbs and sauté over medium heat until toasted.
5. Grate the zest from the lemon and cut the lemon in half to squeeze the juice into the pan (half should be enough).
6. Mix in the salt and black pepper and cook, stirring constantly with a wooden spoon, until dry.
7. Preparing the broccoli:
8. To save extra time, you can cook the broccoli florets right in their microwavable bag. (Or, you can boil them for 4-5 min)
9. Microwave the broccoli according to the packageDirections. (Plot them on a microwave-safe plate and sprinkle with a few tbsps of water if you're using fresh broccoli). Cover with plastic wrap and microwave 3-5 minutes or until crisp-tender.
10. Remove and sprinkle with the Lemon Crumbs and olive oil.

Hearty Red Bell Pepper and Green Bean Toss

A very hearty and delicious way to sneak more vegetables into your diet. This veggie medley goes fantastic with chicken, eggs, fish, and especially steak. This recipe does not use the grill, unless you have cooked vegetables stashed in the fridge ready to go.

Directions:

1. Melt some butter in a skillet and throw in the green beans, bell pepper strips, and remaining ingredients, tossing to evenly coat.
2. Add 1/4 cup water.
3. Cook the vegetables for 4-6 minutes with a lid.
4. Remove the lid and cook, stirring often, 1-2 more minutes or until water is mostly evaporated and the beans are tender.

Ingredients:

2 tbsps butter
2 (8-oz.) packages French green beans
1 red bell pepper, cut into thin strips
3 shallots, sliced
2 garlic cloves, minced
1/2 teaspoon salt
1/8 teaspoon ground red pepper

Creamed Corn

Who doesn't love creamed corn? It's the perfect side dish to serve up with any meal. Very simple and easy to make — a favorite among kids and adults alike. This dish does not use the grill to prepare, apart from the bacon.

Ingredients:

1/4 cup butter or margarine
2 1/2 cups fresh corn kernels
   (about 8 ears)
1/2 cup milk
1 tbsp cornstarch
1 tbsp sugar
1/2 teaspoon salt

Directions:

1. Grab a large skillet and spoon some butter over medium heat.
2. Stir in the corn kernels and milk.
3. Now sprinkle in the cornstarch, sugar, and salt — stir well (this is important!).
4. Bring the entire mixture to a boil, stirring constantly.
5. Reduce heat to a simmer, STILL stirring constantly, for about 10-12 minutes. Serve hot and fresh for best taste.
6. To serve with bacon and leeks:
7. Preheat the grill to medium-high heat.
8. Add the bacon strips until they're crispy (or to your liking)
9. Remove the bacon and chop them into strips.
10. Chop some leeks as well and sprinkle both over the finished dish.

Honey-Glazed Baby Carrots

This dish does not use the grill to prepare. It pairs well with any of the meat recipes in this book because it is straight-up healthy and delicious. It's a perfect side dish to prepare while the chicken or beef is cooking.

Directions:

1. Boil a pot of water in a medium-sized saucepan.
2. Throw in the carrots and cook for 20 min, or until they're tender.
3. Drain the water and mix the carrots and remaining ingredients in a large bow. Mix well.

Ingredients:

1 1/2 quarts water

5 cups baby carrots

3 tbsps chopped fresh parsley

2 tbsps honey

1/2 teaspoon salt

1/2 teaspoon grated orange rind

1/4 teaspoon freshly ground
    black pepper

Perfectly Roasted Sweet Potato Wedges

Finally, who doesn't love fried potatoes? They pretty much go great with just about anything, even by themselves! The best part is that this one is a healthy alternative to the oily fast food ones. Have the potatoes chopped and seasoned to throw them in the grill with your favorite meat for the perfect side.

Ingredients:

2 tbsps olive oil

3 tbsps brown sugar

1/4 teaspoon ground nutmeg

Kosher salt and pepper

4 pounds small sweet potatoes, each peeled and cut into 8 wedges

8 sprigs thyme

Directions:

1. Combine the following ingredients in a large bowl: oil, sugar, nutmeg, 1 teaspoon salt, and 1/2 teaspoon pepper.
2. Throw in the sweet potato wedges and shake vigorously to coat evenly.
3. Preheat the grill to medium-high heat.
4. Place the wedges on the grill and let them cook until they start browning.
5. Flip after about 5-6 min, or until the edges are dark brown and the wedges are crisp.

It's a fact: readers who follow an ACTION GUIDE as they read and use cookbooks tend to have the most success!

Here's what I'm going to do to thank you for downloading my book. Go to the link below to instantly sign up for these bonuses.

Here's just a taste of what subscribers get:

Printable Kitchen Guides:

- Keep your food fresher for longer with the Extra-Long Food Storage Guide
- No more guess work in the kitchen -- Metric Conversion Guide
- Make delicious spreads in minutes -- Easy Spreads Guide
- Protect your family from consuming undercooked meat -- Meat Grilling Guide
- Many more new upcoming high-quality guides

Books and Recipes:

- New mouth-watering recipes you have NEVER tried before
- New books I publish for FREE

GRAB YOUR FREEBIES NOW AT
COOKINGWITHAFOODIE.COM

Made in the USA
San Bernardino, CA
20 March 2017